3-MINUTE
DEVOTIONS

WITH

Andrew Murray

3-MINUTE
DEVOTIONS

WITH

Andrew Murray

180 Readings to Deepen Your Prayer Life

BARBOUR BOOKS
An Imprint of Barbour Publishing, Inc.

© 2015 by Barbour Publishing, Inc.

ISBN 978-1- 68322-130-2

eBook Editions:
Adobe Digital Edition (.epub) 978-1-63409-123-7
Kindle and MobiPocket (.prc) 978-1-63409-124-4

Prayers written by Shanna D. Gregor.

Published by Barbour Books, an imprint of Barbour Publishing, Inc., P.O. Box 719, Uhrichsville, Ohio 44683, www.barbourbooks.com

Our mission is to publish and distribute inspirational products offering exceptional value and biblical encouragement to the masses.

 Member of the
Evangelical Christian
Publishers Association

Printed in the United States of America.

Introduction

A deeper spiritual life cannot grow without deeper daily devotion to God's Word and to prayer. No one knew this better than Andrew Murray. One of the best-loved and most widely read writers on the deeper Christian life, this South African pastor, preacher, and missions speaker prayed for—and witnessed—remarkable spiritual revival on three continents, and every day experienced the need for personal renewal.

If you share that hunger for God's presence, *3-Minute Devotions with Andrew Murray* will satisfy you with an astonishing banquet of riches. Here, thoughtfully chosen from the best of Murray's 240 books and carefully updated in today's language, are his treasured insights on prayer along with simple tools that will help you use them to draw closer to God. A daily scripture selection deepens your insight, while a brief prayer focuses your devotions.

"Time alone with the Lord Jesus each day is indispensable," insisted Andrew Murray. As you begin to satisfy your hunger for God with this inspiring devotional, you won't want to miss a single moment.

*Be careful for nothing; but
in every thing by prayer and
supplication with thanksgiving
let your requests be made known
unto God. And the peace of God,
which passeth all understanding,
shall keep your hearts and
minds through Christ Jesus.*
PHILIPPIANS 4:6–7 KJV

Wait upon God

He [Daniel] prayed three times a day,
just as he had always done, giving thanks to his God.
DANIEL 6:10

The more I think of and pray about the religious situation in our country, the deeper my conviction becomes that Christians do not realize the aim of conversion is to bring them into daily fellowship with the Father in heaven.

For the believer, taking time each day with God's Word and in prayer is indispensable. Each day, we need to wait upon God for His presence and His love to be revealed. It is not enough at conversion to accept forgiveness of sins or even to surrender to God. That is only a beginning. We must understand that we have no power on our own to maintain our spiritual life. We need to receive new grace daily from heaven through fellowship with the Lord Jesus. This cannot be obtained by a hasty prayer or a superficial reading of a few verses from God's Word. We must take time to come into God's presence, to feel our weakness and our need, and to wait on God through His Holy Spirit to renew our fellowship with Him. Then we may expect to be kept by the power of Christ throughout the day.

It is my aim to help Christians see the absolute necessity of spending time with the Lord Jesus. Without this, the joy and power of God's Holy Spirit in daily life cannot be experienced.

Heavenly Father, as I come into Your presence,
I desire to know more of You. Teach me to wait quietly,
with expectation that You will reveal Your love to me.
I surrender all to You, Lord. Amen.

From Day to Day

Though our bodies are dying,
our spirits are being renewed every day.
2 CORINTHIANS 4:16

All Christians, young or old, must learn the absolute necessity of fellowship with Jesus each day. This lesson is not always taught at the beginning of the Christian life. The grace we have received of the forgiveness of sins and of joy in the Holy Spirit can only be preserved by daily renewal in fellowship with Jesus Christ Himself.

Many Christians backslide because this truth is not clearly taught. Some are unable to stand against temptation or their old nature. Though they strive to do their best to fight against sin and to serve God, they have no strength. They have never really grasped the secret that the Lord Jesus will continue His work in the believer every day from heaven. But there is one condition: Time alone with the Lord Jesus each day is the indispensable condition of growth and power. Read Matthew 11:25–30. Listen to Christ's words: "Come to me. . .and I will give you rest. . . . Let me teach you. . .and you will find rest for your souls." Let the Lord teach you just how gentle and humble He is. Bow before Him, tell Him that you need Him and His love, and He will let His love rest on you. This applies not only to young Christians but to all who love the Lord.

Lord, I need You. Renew me each day as I spend one-on-one time with You. Fill me with Your love so that I may overflow with who You are and treat others as You would, Father. Amen.

Fellowship with God

*"I have loved you even as the Father
has loved me. Remain in my love."*

JOHN 15:9

The three persons in the Godhead are the Father, the Son, and the Holy Spirit—each one is different from the others. God desires to reveal Himself as a person. Each one of us is an individual, distinct from others and standing in certain relationships to others. God will reveal Himself to us as a person, and we are called to enter into fellowship with Him.

God greatly desires this relationship with us, but sin has come between us and our God. Even in Christians who know God, there is often great ignorance and even indifference to this personal relationship of love to God.

People believe that at conversion their sins are forgiven, that God accepts them so they may go to heaven, and that they should try to do God's will. But they do not realize, even as a father and his child on earth enjoy being together, they must have this intimate fellowship with God each day.

Our relationship to Christ rests on His deep, tender love to us. We are not capable on our own to render Him this love, but the Holy Spirit will do the work in us. Meditate quietly on this thought: "And because they love me, my Father will love them. And I will love them" (John 14:21). Take time to experience this personal fellowship.

*Lord, I pray that I remain in Your love. May the Father
reveal Himself to me as I fellowship with You and come to
intimately know each person of the Godhead. Amen.*

Jesus

"You are to name him Jesus,
for he will save his people from their sins."

MATTHEW 1:21

The Lord Jesus was a person on this earth. He had His own individual name. His mother, His disciples, all His friends called Him by this name—Jesus. But they probably thought little of what that name meant. Nor do the majority of Christians know what a treasure is contained in that name—Jesus—"He shall save His people from their sins."

Many think about His death on the cross and His resurrection, but do they realize that He is a living person in heaven who thinks of us each day? He wants us to bring Him our love and worship.

When we first ask Jesus Christ to save us from our sins, we know very little about how this is done. The living Christ reveals Himself to us, and through the power of His love, our desire to sin is taken away. Through personal fellowship with Him, Jesus saves us from our sins.

First, we must come to Jesus confessing all the sin in our hearts. We must know Him as the almighty personal Savior in whom God's holiness dwells. As we fellowship together in the expression of mutual love, by the work of His Holy Spirit in our hearts, His love will expel and conquer all the sin.

Jesus, reveal Yourself to me. As I spend time with You,
may the Holy Spirit work mightily in my heart. Thank You
for saving me. I treasure my relationship with You. Amen.

Alone with God

"When you pray, go away by yourself, shut the door
behind you, and pray to your Father in private."
MATTHEW 6:6

Have you ever thought what a wonderful privilege it is to have the liberty of asking God to meet with you and to hear what you have to say? We should use such a privilege gladly and faithfully.

"When you pray," says Jesus, "go away by yourself, shut the door behind you, and pray to your Father in private." This means two things. 1) Shut the world out; withdraw from all the thoughts and concerns of the day. 2) Shut yourself in alone with God to pray in secret. Let this be your chief object in prayer, to realize the presence of your heavenly Father. Let your goal be "Alone with God."

Being alone in His presence and praying to the Father in secret is only the beginning. Come to Him in the full assurance that He knows how you long for His help and guidance. He will listen to you.

Then follows the great promise of verse 6: "Then your Father, who sees everything, will reward you." Your Father will see to it that your prayer is not in vain. Prayer in secret will be followed by the secret working of God in your heart.

God, I shut the world out as I come into Your presence.
I deliberately quiet my mind—setting aside all the things I am
concerned about or need to do today. Consume me with Your
comforting presence and envelop me with Your love. Amen.

The Importance of Faith

"Don't be afraid. Just have faith."
MARK 5:36

This is a lesson of the greatest importance. When praying alone in the presence of God, we must trust implicitly in the love of God and in the power of the Lord Jesus. Take time to ask yourself this question: Is my heart full of a steadfast faith in God's love? If this is not the case, focus on this before you begin to pray. Faith does not come of itself. Consider quietly how impossible it is for God to lie. He is ready with infinite love to give you His blessing. Take some text of scripture in which God's power, faithfulness, and love are revealed. Apply the words and say: "Yes, Lord, I will pray with firm faith in You."

It is a mistake to limit the word *faith* to the forgiveness of sins and to our acceptance as children of God. Faith includes far more. We must have faith in all that God is willing to do for us. We must have faith according to our special needs. Jesus Christ gives grace for each new day, and our faith must reach out according to the needs of the day.

When you enter into the Father's presence and before you begin to pray, ask yourself: Do I really believe that God is here with me and that the Lord Jesus will help me to pray? Jesus often taught His disciples how indispensable faith was to true prayer. He will teach you as well.

God, thank You for the gentle reminder that You are always with me, as You are right now. I trust You to bless me and keep me. I reach out to You in faith, believing You will provide everything I need to navigate life—today and each day that follows. Amen.

Obey the Word of God

*"People do not live by bread alone, but by every word
that comes from the mouth of God."*

MATTHEW 4:4

Bread is indispensable to life. We all understand this. However strong a person may be, if he takes no nourishment, he will grow weaker and eventually die. Even so with the Word of God.

Bread must be eaten. I may know all about bread. I may give it to others. I may have bread in my house and on my table in great abundance, but that will not help me. I must eat the bread. If through illness I am unable to eat it, I shall die. Likewise, mere knowledge of God's Word and even preaching it to others will not help me. It is not enough to think about it. I must feed on God's Word and take it into my heart and life.

Bread must be eaten daily, and the same is true of God's Word. The psalmist says: "They delight in the law of the LORD, meditating on it day and night" (Psalm 1:2). "Oh, how I love your instructions! I think about them all day long" (Psalm 119:97). To secure a strong and powerful spiritual life, spending time in God's Word every day is indispensable. When on earth, the Lord Jesus learned, loved, and obeyed the word of the Father. If you seek fellowship with Him, you will find Him in His Word.

*Heavenly Father, I love Your Word. I feed on it day and night—
meditating on it always. Help me to develop spiritual muscles
that keep me secure and strong in my faith. Amen.*

The Word and Prayer

Restore my life again as you promised.
PSALM 119:107

Prayer and the Word of God are inseparable and should always go together. In His Word, God speaks to me, and in prayer, I speak to God. If there is to be true communication, God and I must both take part. If I simply pray without using God's Word, I am apt to use my own words and thoughts. Taking God's thoughts from His Word and presenting them before Him really gives prayer its power. God's Word is indispensable for all true prayer!

Through the Word, the Holy Spirit shows me who God is. The Word also teaches me how sinful I am. It reveals to me all the wonders that God will do for me and the strength He will give me to do His will. The Word teaches me how to pray—with a strong desire, a firm faith, and constant perseverance. The Word teaches me not only who I am but who I may become. Above all, it reminds me that Christ is the great Intercessor and allows me to pray in His name. Learn to renew your strength each day in God's Word and to pray according to His will.

God, Your Word is life to me. As I come to You in prayer,
You speak to me through Your Word. May You continually
reveal to me the wonders of Your love and grace.
Help me to persevere in prayer. Amen.

Obedience

"If you obey me and do whatever I command you...
I will be your God."

JEREMIAH 11:4

God gave this command to Israel when He gave them the law, but Israel had no power to keep the law. So God gave a "new covenant" to enable His people to live a life of obedience. We read in Jeremiah 32:40: "I will make an everlasting covenant with them.... I will put a desire in their hearts to worship me, and they will never leave me." Ezekiel 36:27 says: "I will put my Spirit in you so that you will follow my decrees and be careful to obey my regulations." These wonderful promises gave the assurance that obedience would be their desire.

Listen to what Jesus says about obedience in John 14:21, 23: "Those who accept my commandments and obey them are the ones who love me. And because they love me, my Father will love them. And I will love them.... And we will come and make our home with each of them."

No father can train his children unless they are obedient. No teacher can teach a child who continues to disobey him. No general can lead his soldiers to victory without prompt obedience. Ask God to imprint this lesson on your heart: The life of faith is a life of obedience. As Christ lived in obedience to the Father, so we need to live in loving obedience to God.

Do you think it's impossible for you to be obedient? It may be impossible for you, but not for God. He has promised to "put my Spirit in you so you will obey my laws." Pray and meditate on these words.

Lord, as You lived in obedience to God, I also choose to live my life in obedience to Him. May my thoughts, choices, words, and heart be in agreement with His will and His Word! Amen.

Confession of Sin

*If we confess our sins to him, he is faithful and just to
forgive us our sins and to cleanse us from all wickedness.*

1 JOHN 1:9

Too often the confession of sin is superficial and neglected. Few
Christians realize how absolutely necessary confession is. An
honest confession of sin gives power to live a life of victory over
sin. We need to confess with a sincere heart every sin that may
be a hindrance in our Christian lives.

Listen to what David says: "I confessed all my sins to you and
stopped trying to hide my guilt. I said to myself, 'I will confess my
rebellion to the LORD.' And you forgave me! All my guilt is gone.
. . . For you are my hiding place; you protect me from trouble.
You surround me with songs of victory" (Psalm 32:5, 7). David
speaks of a time when he was unwilling to confess his sin. "When
I refused to confess my sin, my body wasted away" (verse 3). But
when he had confessed his sin, a wonderful change came.

Confession means not only that I confess my sin with shame
and repentance but that I turn it over to God, trusting Him to
take it away. Such confession implies that I am unable to get rid
of my guilt unless, by an act of faith, I trust God to deliver me.
This deliverance means that I know my sins are forgiven and
that Christ undertakes to cleanse me from the sin and keep me
from its power.

*God, I open my heart to You. Reveal the secret places where sin
tries to hide. Expose each and every area of my life that
I have not fully surrendered to You. Amen.*

The First Love

"But I have this complaint against you.
You don't love me or each other as you did at first!"
Revelation 2:4

In Revelation 2:2-3, eight signs are mentioned showing the zeal of the church at Ephesus, but there was one bad sign. The Lord said: "Turn back to me and do the works you did at first. If you don't repent, I will come and remove your lampstand from its place among the churches" (verse 5). What was this sin? "You don't love me or each other as you did at first!"

We find the same sin in the church today. There is enthusiasm for the truth, there is continuous hard work, but what the Lord values most is missing: tender, fervent love for Him.

A Christian may be a good example in all he does, yet the tender love for Jesus is missing. There is no personal, daily fellowship with Christ. All the many activities with which people satisfy themselves are nothing in the eyes of the Master.

Dear friend, this book speaks of the fellowship of love with Christ and spending time in His presence. Everything depends on this. Christ came from heaven to love us just as the Father loved Him. He suffered to win our hearts for this love. His love can be satisfied with nothing less than deep personal love.

Christ considers this of prime importance. Let us do so, too. Even though we are doing many good things "for the Lord," we must not leave "our first love."

Lord, I love You. Nothing matters more than quiet time
in Your presence. Help me to remain passionate and steadfast
in my love for You. Open my eyes to distractions that
may get in the way of my focus on You. Amen.

The Holy Spirit

*"He will bring me glory by telling you
whatever he receives from me."*

JOHN 16:14

The last night that He was with His disciples, Jesus promised to send the Holy Spirit as a Comforter. Although His bodily presence was removed, they would realize His presence in them and with them in a wonderful way. The Holy Spirit of God would reveal Christ in their hearts so that they would experience His presence with them continually. The Spirit would glorify Christ and would reveal to them the glorified Christ in love and power.

Do not fail to understand, to believe, and to experience this wonderful truth. Doing the Lord's work is not a duty performed in one's own strength. No, that is impossible; it is the Holy Spirit alone who will teach us to love Him sincerely.

God must have entire possession of us. He claims our whole heart and life. He will give us the strength to have fellowship with Christ, to keep His commandments, and to abide in His love. Once we have grasped this truth, we will begin to feel our deep dependence on the Holy Spirit and ask the Father to send Him in power into our hearts.

Holy Spirit, I give my heart to the heavenly Father, and my life shows it. Reveal Christ in my heart so I may be aware of His continual loving presence. Thank You. Amen.

Christ's Love to Us

*"I have loved you even as the Father
has loved me. Remain in my love."*
JOHN 15:9

In relationships between friends and relatives, everything depends on their love to each other. What value is wealth if love is lacking between husband and wife or parents and children? What value is knowledge and enthusiasm in God's work without the knowledge and experience of Christ's love? (See 1 Corinthians 13:1–3.) Christians need to know by experience how much Christ loves them and to learn how they may abide and continue in that love.

Christ says: "As the Father has loved Me"—that is a divine, everlasting, wonderful love! "I also have loved you." The same love with which He had loved the Father He now gives us. He really desires that this everlasting love should rest upon us. What a blessing! Christ wants us to live in the power of the love of God that He also experienced.

In your fellowship with Christ in private or in public, you are surrounded by God's love. Jesus longs to fill you with His love. Read from time to time what God's Word says about the love of Christ. Meditate on the words and let them sink into your heart. Sooner or later, you will begin to realize: the greatest happiness of your life is that you are loved by the Lord Jesus and can live in fellowship with Him every day.

*Lord, thank You for loving me unconditionally. Help me
to live in the power of the love of the heavenly Father.
May I come to love You more and more. And may Your love
overflow from my heart and into the lives of others. Amen.*

Our Love to Christ

You love him even though you have never seen him.
Though you do not see him now, you trust him.

1 PETER 1:8

People who had never seen Christ still truly loved Him and believed in Him. Their hearts were filled with unspeakable joy. Such is the life of a Christian who really loves the Lord.

The chief attribute of the Father and of the Son is love to each other and love to man. This should be the chief characteristic of the true Christian. Life becomes a well of living water, flowing out as love to the Lord Jesus.

This love is not merely a happy feeling. It is an active principle. It takes pleasure in doing the will of the Lord. It is joy to keep His commandments. As the love of Christ was shown to us by His death on the cross, our love must be exhibited in unselfish, self-sacrificing lives. Please understand this: in the Christian life, love to Christ is everything!

Great love results in great faith—faith in His love to us, faith in the powerful revelation of His love in our hearts, faith that He will work all His good pleasure in us. The wings of faith and love will lift us up to heaven, and we shall be filled with joy beyond words. The joy of the Christian is an indispensable witness to the world of the power of Christ to change hearts and to fill them with love and gladness.

Take time daily in His presence to drink in His love.

Lord, I take great pleasure in doing Your will. I set my eyes
on You today, fully focused to live my faith with unselfish
acts of love and kindness. May my actions and
words always point others to You! Amen.

Love to Christians

"So now I am giving you a new commandment:
Love each other."
JOHN 13:34

Jesus told His disciples that as the Father had loved Him, even so He loved them. And now, following His example, we must love one another with the same love. "Your love for one another will prove to the world that you are my disciples" (John 13:35). He had prayed: "I pray that they will all be one. . .as you are in me, Father, and I am in you. And may they be in us so that the world will believe you sent me" (John 17:21). If we exhibit the love that was in God toward Christ, and in Christ to us, the world will be obliged to confess that our Christianity is genuine.

This is what actually happened. The Greeks and Romans, Jews and heathens hated each other. Between all the nations of the world, there was hardly a thought of love. The very idea of self-sacrifice was a strange one. When unbelievers saw that Christians from different nations, under the powerful working of the Holy Spirit, loved one another even to the point of self-sacrifice in times of need—they were amazed. They said: "Behold, how these people love one another!" Often Christ's love is not evident among Christians. Ask God to enable you to love your fellow believers as Christ loves you.

Jesus, relationships are difficult. Those I love most and
who know me best can easily push my buttons. Help me to
draw strength from You, that I may consistently demonstrate
love and kindness in my words and actions. Amen.

Love to Sinners

You can be sure that whoever brings the sinner back
from wandering will save that person from death.
JAMES 5:20

What a wonderful thought—that I may save a sinner from everlasting death. This can happen if I bring that person back to the truth. This is the calling of every Christian.

When Christ and His love took possession of our hearts, He gave us this love that we might bring others to Him. This is how Christ's kingdom is extended. Everyone who has the love of Christ is constrained to tell others. In the early Christian church, people went out and shared the love of Christ. Secular writers have told us that the rapid spread of Christianity in the first century was because each convert tried to bring the good news to others. What a change has come over the church!

Many Christians never try to bring others to Christ. May the time soon come when Christians will feel constrained to share the love of Christ. In a revival in Korea, the converts were filled with such a burning love for Christ that they felt bound to tell others of His love. It was even taken as a test of membership that each one should have brought another to the Lord before being admitted to the church.

Lord, ignite a fire of Your passion in my heart for lost
souls. Help me to seize every opportunity You present
to share with others the gospel of Your great love.
Give me courage to speak boldly for You. Amen.

The Spirit of Love

*For we know how dearly God loves us, because he has
given us the Holy Spirit to fill our hearts with his love.*

ROMANS 5:5

Is it impossible for a Christian to live this life of love? Often we
make little progress in this spirit of love because of our unbelief
and lack of faith in God's promises.

We need continually to remind ourselves that it is not in
our own strength that we can reach the love of Christ. The love
of God is shed abroad in our hearts daily by the Spirit of God. It
is only as we are wholly surrendered to the Spirit that we will be
able to live according to God's will. When the inner life of love
is renewed from day to day, we shall love others.

You can pray with Paul: "When I think of [the wisdom and
scope of God's plan], I fall to my knees and pray to the Father
. . .that from his glorious, unlimited resources he will empower
you with inner strength through his Spirit. Then Christ will
make his home in your hearts as you trust in him. Your roots will
grow down into God's love and keep you strong. And may you
have the power to understand, as all God's people should, how
wide, how long, how high, and how deep his love is" (Ephesians
3:14–18). You may know this love on one condition: you must be
strengthened by the Spirit so that Christ may dwell in your heart.

Take this message from God's Word. Unless you are on your
knees, you cannot live in this love. A life of prayer will make a
life of love to Christ, other Christians, and those without Christ
a reality in your experience.

*Heavenly Father, I cannot love enough on my own. It is
only when I surrender completely to You that I am filled
with Your love and can pass it on to others. Amen.*

Persevering Prayer

Never stop praying.
1 THESSALONIANS 5:17

One of the greatest drawbacks to the life of prayer is that the answer does not come as quickly as we expect. We are discouraged and think: "Perhaps I do not pray right." So we do not persevere. Jesus often talked about this. There may be a reason for the delay, and the waiting may bring a blessing. Our desire must grow deeper and stronger, and we must ask with our whole heart. God puts us into the practicing school of persevering prayer so that our weak faith may be strengthened.

Above all, God wants to draw us into closer fellowship with Him. When our prayers are not answered, we learn that the fellowship and love of God are more to us than the answers of our requests, and then we continue in prayer.

Do not be impatient or discouraged if the answer does not come. "Always be prayerful." "Keep on praying." You will find real blessing in doing so. Ask whether your prayer is really in accordance with the will of God and the Word of God. Ask if it is in the right spirit and in the name of Christ. You will learn that the delay in the answer is one of the most precious ways God gives you His grace.

Those who have persevered before God are those who have had the greatest power in prayer.

*Lord, I resist discouragement and impatience today as
I reach out to You for the fulfillment of promises I've
found in Your Word. Give me strength to persevere—
holding fast to my faith in You—as I wait. Amen.*

The Prayer Meeting

They all met together and were constantly united in prayer....
And everyone present was filled with the Holy Spirit.
ACTS 1:14; 2:4 (SEE ALSO MATTHEW 18:19–20)

In a genuine prayer meeting, God's children meet together, not as in church to listen to one speaker, but to lift up their hearts unitedly to God. Christians are drawn closer to each other. Those who are weak are strengthened and encouraged by the testimony of the older and more experienced members, and young Christians have the opportunity of telling of the joy of the Lord. As a result, God's blessing is poured out at home and abroad.

But there are also dangers to be considered. Some may attend and be edified but never learn to pray themselves. Others go for the religious fervor and have a form of godliness, but they do not know the hidden life of prayer. Unless there is much prayer alone in the presence of God, attendance at a prayer meeting may be a mere ritual.

A "living prayer" meeting will have great influence when its roots are nourished by the life of prayer alone in God's presence. Prayer should include God's people all over the world. As on the day of Pentecost, there must be waiting on God for the filling of the Holy Spirit.

Remember, you do not live for yourself alone but are part of the body of Christ. As the roots of the tree hidden deep in the earth and the branches that spread out to heaven are one, so the hidden prayer life is inseparably bound up with united prayer.

God, as I join my heart and prayers with others, pour out
Your presence. Show us You are near and that You hear the
concerns of Your people. I am thankful for other believers,
Father, who are willing to join me in prayer. Amen.

Intercession

Pray in the Spirit at all times and on every occasion.
EPHESIANS 6:18

Will God really make the pouring out of blessing on others dependent on our prayers? Yes, He makes us His fellow workers. He has taken us into partnership in His work. If we fail to do our part, others will suffer and His work will suffer.

God has appointed intercession as one of the means by which others will be saved and Christians built up in the faith. People all over the world will receive life and blessing through our prayers. Should we not expect God's children to endeavor with all our strength to pray for God's blessing on the world?

Begin to use intercession as a means of grace for yourself and for others. Pray for your neighbors. Pray for sinners that they may come to Christ. Pray for your minister and for missionaries. Pray for your country and for government leaders. If you live a life completely for God, you will realize that the time spent in prayer is an offering pleasing to God.

Yes, "pray in the Spirit at all times. . .and be persistent in your prayers for all believers everywhere." In so doing, you will learn the lesson that intercession is the chief means of bringing others to Christ and bringing glory to God.

Father God, help me recognize the times You call me
to intercession. Fill me with Your words. Help me to
be persistent during these times, not letting go until
You have been glorified. Amen.

Prayer and Fasting

Jesus told them..."But this kind of demon won't
leave except by prayer and fasting."

MATTHEW 17:20-21

Jesus teaches us that a life of faith requires both prayer and fasting. Prayer grasps the power of heaven; fasting loosens the hold on earthly pleasure.

Jesus Himself fasted to get strength to resist the devil. He taught His disciples that fasting should be in secret and the Father would reward it openly. Abstinence from food, or moderation in taking it, helps to focus on communication with God.

Let's remember that abstinence, moderation, and self-denial are a help to the spiritual life. After having eaten a hearty meal, one does not feel much desire to pray. To willingly sacrifice our own pleasure or enjoyment will help to focus our minds more fully on God and His priorities. The very practice needed in overcoming our own desires will give us strength to take hold of God in prayer.

Our lack of discipline in prayer comes from our fleshly desire of comfort and ease. "Those who belong to Christ Jesus have nailed the passions and desires of their sinful nature to his cross and crucified them there" (Galatians 5:24). Prayer is not easy work. For the real practice of prayer—taking hold of God and having communion and fellowship with Him—it is necessary that our selfish desires be sacrificed.

Isn't it worth the trouble to deny ourselves daily in order to meet the holy God and receive His blessings?

*Jesus, I approach You with lifted hands, palms open,
signifying that I have let go of all earthly pleasures and
stand ready to grasp the power of heaven. My life and
my heart are fully surrendered to You. Amen.*

The Spirit of Prayer

For the Spirit pleads for us believers
in harmony with God's own will.
ROMANS 8:27

Prayer is not our work. It is God's work in us by His almighty power. As we pray, our attitude should be one of silent expectation that the Holy Spirit will help in our weakness and pray for us with groanings that cannot be expressed.

What a thought! When I feel how imperfect my prayer is, when I have no strength of my own, I may bow in silence before God in the confidence that His Holy Spirit will teach me to pray. The Spirit is the Spirit of prayer. It is not my work, but God's work in me. The Spirit will make perfect the work even in my weakness.

We see an example of this in the story of Jacob. The same One who wrestled with him and seemed to withhold the blessing was in reality strengthening him to continue and to prevail in prayer. Prayer is the work of the triune God: the Father, who gives the desire and will provide all we need; the Son, who through His intercession teaches us to pray in His name; and the Holy Spirit, who in secret will strengthen our weak desires.

The Spirit of truth will glorify Christ in us, and the Spirit of love will shed this love abroad in our hearts. And we have the Spirit of prayer, through whom our life may be one of continual prayer. Thank God that the Holy Spirit has been given to teach us to pray.

Holy Spirit, teach me to pray. When I don't know what to pray,
fill my heart with the right words. And when I am tempted to fill
my prayer time with complaints, stir my heart to praise. Amen.

Wholly for Christ

*Christ died for everyone so that those who receive his
new life will no longer live for themselves.*

2 CORINTHIANS 5:15

Paul describes here a threefold life. First, the life of the Christian who lives according to his old nature: for himself alone. The second, the life of the true Christian: he lives wholly for Christ. Third, the life of Christ in heaven: He lives wholly for us.

We need to be convinced of the foolishness of living only for ourselves. At conversion, we focus more on our own salvation and less on the claim that Christ has on us. Many Christians continue to live for themselves, content with doing little for the Master. Happiness comes to the believer who realizes the privilege of consecrating one's life entirely to God.

The great hindrance to such a life is the unbelief which says it is impossible. But when the truth takes hold—Christ in heaven lives for me and will impart His life to me—then we know that He will enable us to live wholly for Him.

May this be your earnest desire, your prayer, and your firm expectation: *Christ has not only died for me but lives in heaven to keep me, His purchased possession.* Christ will keep you as a member of His body, to work and live for Him. Pray for grace to live completely for God, whether in sharing with unbelievers or in serving His people. Take time to be united with Christ in prayer so that you can say with all your heart: *I live wholly for Him.*

*Lord, let me not be content living just for myself—only coming
to You when I want or need something. Instead, let my life
be filled with Your presence, always mindful of who
You are and how You love me. Amen.*

The Cross of Christ

My old self has been crucified with Christ.

GALATIANS 2:20

The cross of Christ is His greatest glory. Because He humbled Himself by dying on the cross in our place, God has highly exalted Him. The cross was the power that conquered Satan and sin. As Christians, we share with Christ in the cross. Christ lives in us through the Holy Spirit, and we live as one who has died with Christ.

As we realize the power of Christ's crucifixion, we live as one who has died to the world and to sin. Christ, the Crucified One, lives in us. Jesus said to His disciples: "If any of you wants to be my follower, you must give up your own way, take up your cross, and follow me" (Mark 8:34). They had seen men carrying a cross. They knew that it meant a painful death. All His life, Christ bore His cross—the death sentence that He should die for the world. As Christians, we must bear the cross, acknowledging that we are worthy of death, believing that we are crucified with Christ and that the Crucified One lives in us. "Our old sinful selves were crucified with Christ" (Romans 6:6). "Those who belong to Christ Jesus have nailed the passions and desires of their sinful nature to his cross and crucified them there" (Galatians 5:24). When we have accepted this life of the cross, we will be able to say: "May I never boast about anything except the cross of our Lord Jesus Christ" (Galatians 6:14).

Allow the Holy Spirit to teach you more about this deep spiritual truth.

*Lord, without Your sacrifice on the cross, death was what
I deserved—but because You sacrificed Your life for mine,
I am set free, dead to sin. Help me to accept the reality
of the cross You bore for me. Thank You, Jesus. Amen.*

The World

When you love the world,
you do not have the love of the Father in you.
1 JOHN 2:15

John teaches us what he means by "the world" in 1 John 2:16. He says: "For the world offers only a craving for physical pleasure, a craving for everything we see, and pride in our achievements and possessions. These are not from the Father, but are from this world."

Because all mankind has fallen through sin, we have come under the power of the world and are deceived by the god of this world. The world with its pleasures surrounds the Christian each day with temptations.

This was the case with Eve in the garden of Eden. We find in Genesis the three characteristics John mentions: 1) The lust of the flesh—"The woman saw that the tree was good for food." 2) The lust of the eyes—"It was pleasant to the eyes." 3) The pride of life—"A tree to be desired to make one wise" (Genesis 3:6 KJV). Our life in the world is full of danger—so much to occupy our eyes and our hearts, so much worldly wisdom and knowledge.

So John tells us: "Stop loving this evil world and all that it offers you, for when you love the world, you show that you do not have the love of the Father in you." Just as the Lord called His disciples, He calls us to leave all and follow Him.

Lord, this world has nothing to offer in comparison
to the eternal life You have lovingly provided for me.
Help me to keep my eyes on things above, focused
only on Your purpose and plan for me. Amen.

Put On Christ

*For as many of you as have been
baptized into Christ have put on Christ.*
GALATIANS 3:27 KJV

The word that is here translated "put on" is the same that is used in regard to putting on clothes. We have put on "the new man," and we have the new nature as a garment that is worn so all can see who we are. The Christian is known as one who has put on Christ and exhibits Him in his whole life and character.

Paul says to "put on the Lord Jesus," not only at conversion, but from day to day. As you put on your clothes each day, so the Christian must daily put on the Lord Jesus. In that way, you reflect the image of Jesus, the new person formed in His likeness.

Put on Christ! This must be done by spending time alone in His presence. As my clothes protect me from wind and sun, even so Christ will be my protection and my joy. As I fellowship with Him in prayer, He strengthens me.

Take time to meditate on this wonderful truth. As your clothing is a necessity, let it be equally indispensable for you to "put on" Jesus Christ, to spend time with Him, and to walk with Him all the day. Take the time and the trouble to do this. Your reward will be great.

*Jesus, I take time in Your presence, choosing to "put on"
the new person I am becoming through the gift of Your grace.
Allow me to be a light to others all my days. Amen.*

The Strength of the Christian

A final word: Be strong in the Lord and in his mighty power.
EPHESIANS 6:10

Since we as Christians have no strength of our own, where may we get it? Notice the answer: "Be strong in the Lord and in his mighty power." Paul had spoken of this power in the earlier part of Ephesians (1:17–20). He had prayed to God to give them the Spirit that they might know the greatness of His power which He displayed when He raised Christ from the dead. This is the literal truth: The greatness of His power which raised Christ from the dead works in every believer. We hardly believe it and much less experience it. That is why Paul prays that God would teach us to believe in His almighty power. In Ephesians 3:16–17, Paul asks the Father to strengthen them by His Spirit, that Christ might dwell in their hearts. And then in verse 20: "Now all glory to God, who is able, through his mighty power at work within us, to accomplish infinitely more than we might ask or think."

Read over these scriptures again and pray for God's Spirit to make these words real to you. Believe in the divine power working in you. Pray that the Holy Spirit may reveal it to you. Appropriate the promise that God will show His power in your heart, supplying all your needs. It is clear that much time is needed with the Father and the Son, if you would experience the power of God within you.

Father God, teach me to never doubt Your almighty power.
Strengthen and encourage me in my faith so I stand
in confidence, knowing You are able to accomplish
more than I could ever ask or hope. Amen.

The Whole Heart

With my whole heart have I sought thee.
PSALM 119:10 KJV

Notice how often the psalmist speaks of "all the heart" or the "whole heart": "Search for him with all their hearts" (Psalm 119:2); "I will put them into practice with all my heart" (verse 34); "I obey your commandments with all my heart" (verse 69); "I pray with all my heart" (verse 145). In seeking God, in observing His law, in crying for His help—each time it is with his whole heart.

When we want to be successful in business, we put our whole heart into it. Isn't this even more necessary in the service of a holy God? He is worthy. The whole heart is needed in the service of God when we worship Him.

We often forget this. In prayer, in reading His Word, in seeking to do His will, we fail to say continually: "I have tried my best—with my whole heart—to find You." Let us learn to say: "I desire to seek God and to serve Him with my whole heart."

Meditate and pray about this. Spend time before God until you know that you really mean what you say and you have the assurance that God will hear your prayer. Then each morning as you approach God in prayer, you can honestly say, "I seek You with my whole heart." You gradually will feel the need of waiting in holy stillness upon God so that He may take possession of your whole heart. You will learn to love Him with your whole heart and your whole mind.

God, as I wait in stillness before You, teach me what it means to search for You and find You. Show me how to seek You with my whole heart so that I may serve You with all that is within me! Amen.

Blessed Reality

God has united you with Christ Jesus.
1 CORINTHIANS 1:30

During His last day with His disciples, the Lord Jesus made several references to being "in Christ Jesus." "When I am raised to life again, you will know that I am in my Father, and you are in me, and I am in you" (John 14:20). Following that in 15:5: "Those who remain in me, and I in them, will produce much fruit." "If you remain in me and my words remain in you, you may ask for anything you want, and it will be granted!" (15:7). We cannot apply these promises unless we first prayerfully accept the words "in Christ."

Paul expressed the same thought in Romans 6:4: "We. . .were buried with Christ." "You also should consider yourselves to be dead to the power of sin and alive to God through Christ Jesus" (verse 11). "There is no condemnation for those who belong to Christ Jesus" (Romans 8:1). And in Ephesians 1:3: "All praise to God. . .who has blessed us with every spiritual blessing in the heavenly realms because we are united with Christ." Colossians 2:9: "For in Christ lives all the fullness of God in a human body." Colossians 2:6: "Just as you accepted Christ Jesus as your Lord, you must continue to follow him." Colossians 4:12: ". . .asking God to make you strong and perfect, fully confident that you are following the whole will of God."

By faith, take hold of the truth that "God establishes us in Christ" and then follow the leading of the Spirit in prayer.

Christ Jesus, I have been established in You. I choose to live in obedience to Your will. Make me strong and perfect, fully confident in the Father's will for my life, as I live each day to bring glory and honor to You. Amen.

Christ in Me

Examine yourselves to see if your faith is genuine.

2 CORINTHIANS 13:5

Christ is in me. What a difference it would make if we could take time every morning to focus on the thought: *Christ is in me.* Christ made it clear to His disciples. The Spirit would teach them: "When I am raised to life again, you will know that I am in my Father, and you are in me, and I am in you" (John 14:20). Through the power of God, we who believe were crucified with Christ and raised again with Him. As a result, Christ is in us! Through faith in God's Word, the Christian accepts it.

Paul expresses this thought in the prayer of Ephesians 3:16: "I pray that from his glorious, unlimited resources he will empower you with inner strength through his Spirit." Notice that it is not the ordinary gift of grace but a special revelation of the riches of His love that Christ may dwell in your heart by faith. Have you been able to grasp that?

Paul said: "I fall to my knees and pray to the Father" (Ephesians 3:14). That is the only way to obtain the blessing. Take time in prayer in His presence to realize "Christ dwells in me." Even in the midst of your daily schedule, look upon your heart as the dwelling place of the Son of God. Then Christ's words:—"Those who remain in me, and I in them, will produce much fruit" (John 15:5)—will become your daily experience.

Christ, I choose to remain in You each day—as You have promised to dwell in me. Even as I go about the practical, little things of life, remind me that my heart is Your home. And everywhere I go, You go, Jesus. Amen.

Christ Is All

Christis all that matters, and he lives in all of us.
COLOSSIANS 3:11

Christ is all—in the eternal counsel of God, in the redemption on the cross, as King on the throne in heaven and on earth. In the salvation of sinners, in the building up of Christ's body, in the care for individuals—Christ is all. Every hour and every day, this knowledge provides comfort and strength to the child of God.

You feel too weak, too unworthy, too untrustworthy. But if you will only accept the Lord Jesus in childlike faith, you have a guide who will supply all your needs. Believe the word of our Savior in Matthew 28:20: "And be sure of this: I am with you always," and you will experience His presence each day.

However cold and dull your feelings may be, however sinful you are, meet the Lord Jesus in secret and He will reveal Himself to you. Tell Him how miserable you really are and then trust Him to help and sustain you.

Each day as you spend time in His presence, let this thought be with you: *Christ is all.* Make it your goal: *Christ is all—to teach me to pray, to strengthen my faith, to give me the assurance of His love, to give me direct access to the Father, and to make me strong for the schedule of the day.*

Lord, I accept You with childlike faith, trusting and believing Your Word. Reveal Yourself to me. Show me Your ways. Lead me in Your truth. You are my everything, all I will ever need! Amen.

The Love of God

God is love, and all who live in love live in God,
and God lives in them.

1 JOHN 4:16

The love of God—what an unfathomable mystery! Jesus said: "There is only One who is good" (Matthew 19:17). The glory of God in heaven is that He wills to do all that is good. That includes the two meanings of the word: good—all that is right and perfect; good—all that makes happiness.

The God who wills nothing but good is a God of love. He does not demand His own way. He does not live for Himself but pours out His love on all living creatures. All created things share in this love so that they may be satisfied with that which is good.

A characteristic of love is that it "does not demand its own way" (1 Corinthians 13:5). It finds happiness in giving to others. It sacrifices itself wholly for others. God offered Himself to mankind in love in the person of His Son, and the Son offered Himself upon the cross to bring that love to men and women. The everlasting love with which the Father loved the Son is the same love with which the Son loves us.

The love of God to His Son, the love of the Son to us, the love with which we love the Son, the love with which we love each other and try to love all men—all is the same eternal, incomprehensible, almighty love of God. Love is the power of the Godhead in the Father, Son, and Holy Spirit.

God, the fact that You love me "no matter what" is difficult
to comprehend; yet I know You love me unconditionally.
There is nothing that can separate me from You. Thank You
for pouring out Your everlasting love on me! Amen.

The Love of Christ

Christ's love controls us.
2 CORINTHIANS 5:14

God sent His Son into the world to let us know His everlasting love, even as it was known in heaven. Even the angels in heaven are filled with praise and worship because of God's love. God's desire is that on this sinful earth His love would take possession of the hearts of men and women.

In order to reveal His love and win our hearts to Himself, God sent Christ, the Son of His love, to earth. The Lord Jesus Christ became man and, even though He was God, humbly made Himself nothing. In His dealings with the poor, the unbelieving, and the rebellious—and through His miracles—He poured out His love into the hearts of sinful men.

God gave the greatest proof of love that the world has ever seen. On the cross, He took our sins upon Himself. He bore the suffering and the scorn of His enemies so that friend and foe alike might know God's eternal love.

Then, after He had ascended to heaven, He gave the Holy Spirit to shed abroad this love in our hearts. Impelled by the love of Christ, the disciples, in turn, offered their lives to make this love known to others.

Think about this. God longs to have our hearts filled with His love so that He can use us as channels for this love to flow out to others. Let us be satisfied with nothing less and sacrifice everything to secure a place for this love in the hearts of men and women.

Heavenly Father, fill my heart with Your love. May Your love overflow from my heart to the hearts of others. I pray that my words and actions shine with Your love so others can experience You through me. Amen.

The Love of the Spirit

He has given us the Holy Spirit to fill our hearts with his love.
ROMANS 5:5

As God's children, we must confess that we know very little of fervent, childlike love for our heavenly Father. Why is this? Perhaps we have not learned the lesson that there must be a constant renewal of faith in what God is able to do. We try to stir up love toward God in our hearts. Yet, in our own strength, we cannot awaken the slightest love to God.

Child of God, believe that the love of God will work as the power in your heart that enables you to love God and to love others. Cease to expect love in yourself. Believe in the power of God's love resting on you and teaching you to love God with His own love.

Learn the lesson of our text: "He has given us the Holy Spirit to fill our hearts with his love." The Spirit will enable us to love God, our friends, and even our enemies. Be assured of two things. First, in your own strength, you cannot love God or your fellow Christians. And second, the Holy Spirit is within you every day and every hour, seeking to fill you with the Spirit of love. Each morning, as you commit yourself into the keeping of the Holy Spirit, let this prayer arise: *Lord, grant me the assurance that You will pour forth the love of Christ into my own heart and then let it stream forth to all around me! Amen.*

Father, I am so thankful that I don't have to love others with my own strength. Instead, the Holy Spirit has filled my heart with love for them. Thank You for the blessing of Your amazing love, God. Amen.

The Power of Love

Overwhelming victory is ours through Christ, who loved us.
ROMANS 8:37

In days of uncertainty, strong racial feelings, and unrest, we need to experience the love of God. Let us anchor our hope in the truth "God is love." God's power, by which He rules the world, is the power of undying love. He works through the hearts and wills of men and women who are wholly yielded to Him. He waits for us to open our hearts to Him in love. Then, full of courage, we become witnesses for Him.

This is how Christ's kingdom is manifested and His reign of love on earth began. Christ died in order to establish this kingdom. The only means He used to gain influence was by showing a serving, suffering love. He saw the possibility of redemption in even the worst of people, knowing that their hearts could never resist the steady influence of love. It was in the fervor of that love that Jesus' disciples were able to do the impossible.

The spirit of hatred and bitterness can never be overcome by argument or reproaches. Some think things can never be different, but if we really believe in the omnipotence of God's love, we may trust His power. Our faith in love as the greatest power in the world should prepare us for a life of communion with God in prayer and for a life of service.

God, I believe in the invincibility of Your love. I trust in Your power. Let Your love flow—every day—to me and through me, into the hearts of others, so that they are unable to resist the steady influence of Your love! Amen.

The Sign of a True Church

*"Your love for one another will prove
to the world that you are my disciples."*

JOHN 13:35

We are taught in most of our creeds that the true church is to be found where God's Word is faithfully and accurately preached and the sacraments are dispensed as instituted by Christ. Christ Himself takes a much broader view. To Him, the distinguishing mark of His followers is not merely what the church teaches—but how we live our lives showing love to each other.

Jesus' death on the cross was love at its highest. We owe everything to this love. Love is the power that moved Christ to die for us. In love, God highly exalted Him as Lord and Christ. Love is the power that broke our hearts, and love is the power that heals them. Love is the power through which Christ dwells and works in us. Love can change my nature and enable me to surrender to God. It gives me strength to live a holy, joyous life, full of blessing to others. Every Christian should show the love of God.

Many Christians are sure it is impossible to lead such a life, and they do not even greatly desire it. They do not understand that we may and can love with God's own love.

If we fully believe that the Holy Spirit, dwelling within us, will maintain this heavenly love from hour to hour, we will be able to understand the words of Christ: "Anything is possible if a person believes" (Mark 9:23). Then we will be able to love God with all our heart, to love family and friends and even our enemies.

*Lord, let my life shine as a beacon, inviting strangers and
friends into the truth of Your love. Change my nature by
the power of Your love, and fill me with a great desire
to demonstrate love against all odds. Amen.*

Race Hatred

Once we, too, were foolish and disobedient. We were misled and became slaves to many lusts and pleasures.

TITUS 3:3

Our text paints a dark picture of the state of human nature! What causes such a sad condition? The answer is "Adam's fall." Think how Cain, the first child born of the man God created, shed the blood of his brother Abel. The first child born on earth came under the power of the devil, who "was a murderer from the beginning" (John 8:44). "The LORD observed the extent of human wickedness on the earth, and he saw that everything they thought or imagined was consistently and totally evil" (Genesis 6:5). No wonder He destroyed mankind by a flood.

Humanity's love of their own people, implanted in their hearts by nature, soon changed to hatred of other peoples. Love of country became the source of race hatred and bloodshed. Note how God has placed the races side by side to see if our Christianity will enable us to overcome race hatred. Will we, in the power of Christ's love, prove that "In this new life, it doesn't matter if you are a Jew or a Gentile, circumcised or uncircumcised, barbaric, uncivilized, slave, or free. Christ is all that matters, and he lives in all of us" (Colossians 3:11)?

What an opportunity there is for the church to prove the power of God's love to change race hatred into brotherly love! God has abundant power to make this happen. As Christians, we need to pray for ourselves and for each other that we would obey the Word of God and live in the power of Christ's love.

Heavenly Father, every single person has the potential to become my brother or sister in Christ. Help me to see every single human being as someone You love deeply and care for immensely. Amen.

Love Your Enemies

"You have heard the law that says,
'Love your neighbor' and hate your enemy."
MATTHEW 5:43

Religious teachers in Christ's day judged that they had a right to say this [Matthew 5:43] because of Leviticus 19:17–18: "Do not nurse hatred in your heart for any of your relatives. Confront people directly so you will not be held guilty for their sin. Do not seek revenge or bear a grudge against a fellow Israelite, but love your neighbor as yourself." They argued that it was only their own people whom they may not hate; it was all right to hate their enemies. But our Lord said: "Love your enemies! Pray for those who persecute you!" (Matthew 5:44).

How often we as Christians follow the example of those religious leaders! The new commandment to love requires much grace, costs time, and needs much earnest prayer.

When I was a minister in Cape Town, I met a German deaconess. She had a class for several Kaffirs who were preparing to join the church. One evening, she spoke about loving our enemies. She asked one man if his people had enemies. "Oh yes!" "Who are they?" "The Fingoes." She asked if he could love a Fingo. His answer was decided. "I can't love Fingo." She told him in that case he could not go to the Communion. He seemed very downcast. He was not received into the church with the others but continued to attend the class. Then one evening, he appeared with a bright face and said, "I now love Fingo." He had prayed about it; God heard his prayer and enabled him to love his enemy.

There is only one way we can love our enemies: by the love of Christ, sought and found in prayer.

Father God, I want to love my enemies. Teach me by
Your grace and mercy how to love those who despise
me and those who desire to do me harm. Help me to
demonstrate Your love to my enemies, Father. Amen.

As God Forgives

*"And forgive us our sins, as we forgive
those who sin against us."*

LUKE 11:4

The forgiveness of sins is the one great gift that sets the sinner free. Forgiveness gives us boldness toward God and is the source of our salvation. The forgiveness of sins gives us a reason to be thankful every day of our lives.

As we walk with God in the assurance of sins forgiven, He desires that we should live as those who have been freely forgiven. We can only prove our sincerity by forgiving those who have offended us as willingly as God has forgiven us.

In the Lord's Prayer, we are taught to pray: "Forgive us our sins—just as we forgive those who have sinned against us." Then at the end: "But if you refuse to forgive others, your Father will not forgive your sins" (Matthew 6:15). In Matthew 18:21, we have the question of Peter: "Lord, how often should I forgive someone who sins against me?" Our Lord answered, "Seventy times seven!"

Then follows the parable of the servant whose lord forgave him his debt but who would not show compassion to his fellow servant. His lord asked: "Shouldn't you have mercy on your fellow servant, just as I had mercy on you?" (Matthew 18:33). So the servant was sent to prison. The Lord warns us: "That's what my heavenly Father will do to you if you refuse to forgive your brothers and sisters from your heart" (Matthew 18:35).

*Lord, sometimes it's really hard to forgive. The memory
of the hurt and pain often keeps me stuck. But by faith
I will obey Your command. Today I choose to forgive,
and I trust that my feelings will follow. Amen.*

The Two Leaders

I urge you, first of all, to pray for all people. Ask God to help them; intercede on their behalf, and give thanks for them.
1 TIMOTHY 2:1

At the time of the unveiling of the Women's Monument at Bloemfontein, South Africa, I spoke a few words about the suffering, praying, all-conquering love of these women. They prayed that God would help them love their enemies and keep them from hatred. I expressed the hope that the feeling of peace and unity might continue and this prayerful love be ours. I said that there were some who feared disunion, not only between the two races in the country, but between those who were of the same race. Not long after, we heard that there had been a breach between the leaders of the two parties.

I felt impelled to write an article on the question: "For whom do you pray?" Someone answered: "I pray for the man at the head of my party who, under God's guidance, has now become the leader of all South Africa." And another: "I pray especially for the man who has brought the interests of my people into the foreground." Would it not be sad if we came into God's presence divided into two camps, praying one against the other? We must pray both for our leaders and for all who are in authority. As leaders of the people, their influence for good or evil is inexpressible. Their hearts are in God's hands, and He can turn them wherever He wills. Let us pray to God in all sincerity for our leaders, that God will grant what is good for the whole land.

God, I pray for the leader of our country. Give him wisdom and discernment and a heart to follow You. Keep him in all his ways so that he may make wise decisions. Amen.

Love and Prayer

Be earnest and disciplined in your prayers. Most important of all, continue to show deep love for each other.
1 PETER 4:7–8

Earnest prayer and fervent love are closely linked. If we pray only for ourselves, we will not find it easy to be in the right attitude toward God. But when our hearts are filled with love for others, we will continue to pray for them, even for those with whom we do not agree.

Prayer holds an important place in the life of love; they are inseparably connected. If you want your love to increase, forget yourself and pray for God's children. If you want to increase in prayerfulness, spend time loving those around you, helping to bear their burdens.

There is a great need for earnest, powerful intercessors! God desires His children to present themselves each day before the throne of grace to pray down the power of the Spirit upon all believers. Unity is strength. Spiritual unity will help us to live unselfishly, wholly for God and others. Let us apply Peter's words to our lives—"earnest in prayer. . .showing deep love for each other."

As we meditate on love to those around us, we will be drawn into fellowship with God. This will come, not by reading or thinking, but by spending time with the Father and with the Lord Jesus through the Holy Spirit. Love leads to prayer—to believing prayer is given the love of God.

Lord, help me to be more aware of the burdens of others. Show me ways I can help shoulder their load and express love and compassion. Remind me to pray for them and their hurts each day. Thank You, Jesus. Amen.

The First Commandment

*"The Lord your God will change your heart. . .so that
you will love him with all your heart and soul."*

Deuteronomy 30:6

God greatly desires our love. It is the nature of all love to want
to be acceptable and to be accepted. God longs to have the love
of our whole heart.

How can we love God with all our heart and soul? In the
same way that we receive salvation—through faith alone. Paul
says, "I live in this earthly body by trusting in the Son of God,
who loved me and gave himself for me" (Galatians 2:20). When
we take time to wait upon God and remember how God sought
to win our love through the gift of His Son, we shall realize that
God has a strong longing for our love.

Our hearts are blind. It is easy to forget that God longs for
the love of His child. Once we believe it, we will feel constrained
to wait before God and ask Him to let His light shine into our
hearts. As the sun gives us its light, God is a thousand times more
willing to give us the light of His love.

As we wait silently before God, we become strong in the
assurance of faith. God, who longs for our love, is almighty and
will fill us with His love by the Holy Spirit.

Take time each day to love God and believe Him with firmer
faith. God will work within us, granting the desire to love Him with
our whole heart. He will enable us to prove our love by keeping
His commandments.

*God, I love You, and today I show my love by spending time
with You. I will meditate on Your Word and quietly
commune with You. Fill me with Your love. Amen.*

Pray for Love

And may the Lord make your love for one another and for all
people grow and overflow, just as our love for you overflows.
1 Thessalonians 3:12

Paul gives us a powerful prayer in this text: that the Lord would make them abound in love toward each other, so that their hearts would be without blame. Without love, true holiness is impossible. Let us use this prayer often.

In 2 Thessalonians 3:5, we read: "May the Lord lead your hearts into a full understanding and expression of the love of God." That is what the Lord Jesus will do for us. As the apostle makes love the chief thing, let us do the same.

"I want you to know how much I have agonized for you . . . . I want [you] to be encouraged and knit together by strong ties of love. I want [you] to have complete confidence that [you] understand God's mysterious plan, which is Christ himself" (Colossians 2:1–2). Paul considers love indispensable for growth in the knowledge of God. God's love can only be experienced when Christians are knit together in love and live for others, not only for themselves.

Take time to meditate on these prayers of Paul. As the sun freely gives its light to the grass that it may grow, so God is more than willing to give His love to us. As you pray and ponder these words, you will gain a strong assurance of what God is able to do for you. He will make you to abound in love and strengthen you to live before Him in holiness and love for others.

Lord Jesus, I ask today that Your love grow within me.
May my heart fill to bursting with love for others,
just as my love overflows for You. Amen.

Song of Love

*Three things will last forever—faith,
hope, and love—and the greatest of these is love.*

1 CORINTHIANS 13:13

Today is wholly devoted to the praise of love. The first three verses of 1 Corinthians 13 speak of the absolute necessity of love as the chief thing in our religion. "If I could speak all the languages of earth and of angels. . .if I had the gift of prophecy . . .if I had such faith that I could move mountains. . .if I gave everything I have to the poor and even sacrificed my body. . .but if I didn't love others," then, three times repeated, "I would only be a noisy gong or a clanging cymbal. . . . I would be nothing. . . . I would have gained nothing." If I have not love, I am of no value.

There are fifteen things said about love, but one sentence sums up its whole nature: "[Love] does not demand its own way" (verse 5). And again: "Love will last forever!" (verse 8). Prophecies, unknown languages, and knowledge will vanish away. Even faith and hope shall be changed into sight. But love lasts forever.

"Love does not demand its own way." Think and pray about this. "Love will last forever." Consider all that means. "The greatest of these is love." Let this love rule in your life.

God is love. "God is love, and all who live in love live in God, and God lives in them" (1 John 4:16). Let your heart be filled with love so that, by God's almighty power, you may be a witness to the transforming power of love. Then you will be a blessing to all around you.

*Lord, I am guilty of wanting things to be my way. I get stuck
thinking that my way is best. Forgive me. Help me instead to
embrace Your way, which is the path of love. Thank You. Amen.*

Like Christ

"I have given you an example to follow.
Do as I have done to you."
JOHN 13:15

The love of Christ is the basis not only of our salvation but also of our daily life and conduct. Jesus clearly says: "Do as I have done to you." The love of Christ is my only hope of salvation. Walking in that love is the way to enjoy that salvation.

"We should help others do what is right and build them up in the Lord. Accept each other just as Christ has accepted you so that God will be given glory" (Romans 15:2, 7). God will work within us to "accept each other just as Christ has accepted [us]."

"Imitate God. . .in everything you do, because you are his dear children. Live a life filled with love, following the example of Christ. He loved us and offered himself as a sacrifice for us" (Ephesians 5:1-2). Paul reminds us that love is everything. Christ loved us so much He died on the cross so we could be God's dear children. It follows that we should walk in love. Those who keep close to Christ will walk in love.

"Since God chose you to be the holy people he loves, you must clothe yourselves with tenderhearted mercy. . . . Make allowance for each other's faults, and forgive anyone who offends you. Remember, the Lord forgave you, so you must forgive others. Above all, clothe yourselves with love, which binds us all together in perfect harmony" (Colossians 3:12-14). As we walk in fellowship with Him, we are given strength to be like Him!

Lord, do a great work within my heart—so I will be
more accepting of others. When I meet people who are
different in thought or deed, help me to be giving and kind,
while modeling Your love and compassion. Amen.

The Power of God's Word

"The very words I have spoken to you are spirit and life."
JOHN 6:63

Frequently, the question is asked: Why do God's children often fail to realize the great value and absolute necessity of loving each other? One answer is unbelief. Without faith, there can be no thought of the power of love within us. True faith acknowledges God's loving care for us and His power to work wonders in our hearts.

It is necessary to be deeply convinced of our total inability to produce this love on our own. We must have a burning desire to receive this heavenly love into our hearts—a love that is holy and can conquer sin and unbelief. When we gain an insight into what God's Word is—a living power in our hearts—we will be filled with the love of God by the Holy Spirit, living and working within us.

Are we ready to acknowledge our deep sinfulness and yield our hearts unreservedly for this love to take possession of us? Are we ready to take time in God's presence in the confidence that His Word will work in us as a seed of new life? If so, then we will love Jesus and each other with a love like God's love for us.

Heavenly Father, forgive my sins as I surrender my heart completely to You. I pray that Your love possesses every part of me. I believe Your Word. May it build confidence in my faith today. Amen.

The Love That Suffers

Live a life filled with love, following the example of Christ.
He loved us and offered himself as a sacrifice for us.
EPHESIANS 5:2

It is strange that love, which is the source of the greatest happiness, should also be the cause of the most intense suffering. Suffering always follows when love seeks to save the object of its love. It is only by suffering that love can gain its end and so attain the highest happiness.

Even the almighty power of God's love could not achieve its purpose without suffering. By suffering, Christ bore the sins of the whole world. Love in the midst of suffering manifested the greatest glory and attained its end perfectly.

Love worthy of the name manifests itself in a life of continual self-sacrifice. Love gives strength to endure, whatever the circumstances.

Loving others may mean tears, heartache, and much persevering in prayer; but love overcomes all obstacles.

Do you long to know the love of Christ in all its fullness? Then yield yourself to Him. Think of yourself as a channel through which the highest love can reach its aim. Begin to suffer with and intercede for those around you. Eventually, you will realize what this life of love is: to live wholly for the welfare and happiness of others.

Lord, relationships are hard, but You know that. When my feelings are hurt or my heart is wounded by someone I love, help me to persevere in prayer and allow Your love to overcome all obstacles standing in my way. Amen.

The Lack of Prayer

Yet you don't have what
you want because you don't ask God for it.
JAMES 4:2

Recently, I attended several conventions at which prayer was often the subject of conversation. A businessman said that the spirit of intercession is what the church of our day needs. Everywhere, people confessed, "We pray too little!" Yet there seemed to be a fear that, because of pressure from work and the force of habit, it was almost impossible to hope for change. Such thinking can only hinder our own joy and our power in God's service.

Dr. Whyte of Edinburgh said that, as a young minister, he thought any time left over from pastoral visitation ought to be spent with his books. He wanted to feed his people with the very best he could prepare. But now he had learned that prayer was more important than study. He felt as if it were almost too late to regain what he had lost and urged us to pray more. What a solemn confession and warning: We pray too little!

Is the call of God for our time and attention more important than our work? If God is waiting to meet us and to give us power from heaven for His work, it is shortsighted to put other work in His place. If there is to be a significant experience of God's presence, there must be more definite and persevering prayer.

God, give me a deep understanding of persevering in prayer.
Prayer is ultimately where the power to persevere in life
comes from, Father. Let me hold fast to You in faith,
unwavering in my communication with You. Amen.

Time for Prayer

Yet no one calls on your name or pleads with you for mercy.
ISAIAH 64:7

At a ministerial meeting, the superintendent of a large district said: "I rise in the morning and have half an hour with God. I am occupied all day with numerous engagements. Not many minutes elapse without my breathing a prayer for guidance. After work, I speak to God of the day's work. But I know little of the intense prayer of which scripture speaks."

There are earnest Christians who have just enough prayer to maintain their spiritual position but not enough to grow spiritually. Seeking to fight off temptation is a defensive attitude, rather than an assertive one which reaches for higher attainment. The scriptural teaching to cry out day and night in prayer must, to some degree, become our experience if we are to be intercessors.

A man said to me, "I see the importance of much prayer, and yet my life hardly allows time for it. Am I to give up? How can I accomplish what I desire?"

I admitted that the difficulty was universal and quoted a Dutch proverb: "What is heaviest must weigh heaviest." The most important must have the first place. The law of God is unchangeable. In our communication with heaven, we only get as we give. Unless we are willing to pay the price—to sacrifice time and attention and seemingly necessary tasks for the sake of the heavenly gifts—we cannot expect much power from heaven in our work.

Lord, I realize everyone has the same number of hours in a day.
It's not that I don't have time to pray—but when I fail to
talk to You, it's because I've chosen to spend my time
doing something else. Please forgive me! Amen.

Finding the Root Cause

And God will generously provide all you need.
Then you will always have everything you need
and plenty left over to share with others.

2 CORINTHIANS 9:8

I met a clergyman who used the expression "the distraction of business." It was one of the greatest difficulties he had to deal with. Every day, he had to visit four different offices in his town. In addition, his predecessor left him the responsibility of several committees where he was expected to do all the work. Everything conspired to keep him from prayer.

Various difficulties make a full prayer life almost impossible. But thank God the things which are impossible with men are possible with God! God's call to prayer need not be a burden nor a cause of guilt. He means for it to be a joy. Through prayer, He can give us strength for all we do and bring down His power to work through us in the lives of others.

Let us confess the sin that shames us and then confront it in the name of our Redeemer. The same light that shows us our sin and condemns us for it will show us the way out of it. Deficiency in our Christian life is the root cause of unfaithfulness in prayer. God will use this discovery to bring us both the power to pray that we long for and also the joy of a new and healthy life, of which prayer is the spontaneous expression.

Father God, through prayer You give me strength. It is Your power working in me that allows me to live for and to love others. Let my prayers be constant, as well as spontaneous, each and every day! Amen.

Health for the Soul

He was amazed to see that no one
intervened to help the oppressed.
ISAIAH 59:16

How can our lack of prayer be transformed into a blessing? How can it be changed into the path where evil may be conquered? How can our relationship with the Father become one of continual prayer?

We must begin by going back to God's Word to study the place God intends for prayer to have in the life of His child. A fresh understanding of what prayer is and what our prayers can be will free us from our wrong attitudes concerning the absolute necessity of continual prayer.

We need insight into how reasonable this divine appointment is. We need to be convinced of how it fits in with God's love and our happiness. Then we will be freed from the false impression of prayer being an arbitrary demand. We will yield to it and rejoice in it as the only way for the blessing of heaven to come to earth. It will no longer be a task and burden of self-effort and strain. As simple as breathing is in the physical life, so will praying be in the Christian life that is led by the Spirit.

Our failure in the prayer life is a result of our failure in the spirit life. Any thought of praying more and of praying effectively will be in vain unless we are brought into closer intimacy with our Lord. His life of prayer on earth and of intercession in heaven is breathed into us in the measure that our surrender and our faith allow.

Lord, let my day be filled with divine appointments
with You. May I live in an atmosphere of perpetual
prayer. As I breathe in and out, let my communication
be a natural exchange with You. Amen.

Ministration of the Spirit and Prayer

"If you sinful people know how to give good gifts to your children, how much more will your heavenly Father give the Holy Spirit to those who ask him."

LUKE 11:13

Jesus said: "Keep on asking, and you will be given what you ask for." God's giving is inseparably connected with our asking. He applied this principle especially to the Holy Spirit. As surely as a father gives bread to his child, so God gives the Holy Spirit to those who ask. The whole ministration of the Spirit is ruled by the one great law: God must give; we must ask. When the Holy Spirit was poured out at Pentecost, it was in answer to prayer.

Along with our confession of the lack of prayer, we also need an understanding of the place prayer occupies in God's plan of redemption. Nowhere is this clearer than in the first half of Acts. The outpouring of the Holy Spirit at the birth of the church is the true measure of the presence of the Spirit.

The Spirit came in answer to prayer. "They all met together and were constantly united in prayer." Then there follows: "On the day of Pentecost, all the believers were meeting together in one place. . . . And everyone present was filled with the Holy Spirit. . . . Those who believed. . .were. . .added to the church that day—about 3,000 in all" (Acts 1:14; 2:1, 4; 2:41).

The Holy Spirit had been promised by Christ. He sat down on His throne and received the Spirit from the Father. But one more thing was needed: the ten days of united, continued supplication of the disciples.

Father, thank You for answered prayer. Thank You for giving when I ask. And although Your response is not always immediate, I know that You are at work behind the scenes on my behalf. Amen.

Spiritual Roots

After this prayer, the meeting place shook,
and they were all filled with the Holy Spirit.
ACTS 4:31

Definite, determined prayer is what we need. Peter and John had been threatened with punishment. When they returned to their friends, they lifted up their voices to God with one accord. When they prayed, "the meeting place shook. . . . They preached the word of God with boldness."

It is as if the story of Pentecost is repeated (the prayer, the filling with the Spirit, the speaking God's Word with boldness) in order to imprint permanently on the church that it is prayer that lies at the root of the spiritual life and power of the church. The degree to which God gives His Spirit is determined by our asking.

Later, people complained about the neglect of the Grecian Jews in the distribution of alms. The apostles proposed the appointment of deacons to serve the tables. "Then we apostles can spend our time in prayer and teaching the word" (Acts 6:4). There is nothing in honest business that prevents fellowship with God. Least of all should ministering to the poor hinder the spiritual life. And yet the apostles felt it would hinder their ministry of prayer and the Word.

What does this teach? Maintenance of the spirit of prayer is possible in many kinds of work, but it is not enough for those who are the leaders of the church. They need to communicate with the King and keep the heavenly world in clear focus for the maintenance of their own spiritual life and also for those around them.

God, thank You for Your Spirit who teaches me to pray.
It is prayer that brings forth the spiritual life and power
of the church. Create in me a fresh, deep desire to
pray fervently, like I never have before. Amen.

Higher Gift

*"Your prayers and gifts to the poor have
been received by God as an offering!"*

Acts 10:4

At Samaria, Philip had preached with great blessing and many believed. But the Holy Spirit had not yet fallen on them. The apostles sent Peter and John to pray for them that they might receive the Holy Spirit.

The power for such prayer was a higher gift than preaching. It was the work of men who had been in closest contact with the Lord. Of all the gifts of the early church, there is none more needed than the gift of prayer. This power is given to those who say, "We will give ourselves to prayer."

The outpouring of the Holy Spirit in the house of Cornelius provides another testimony to the interdependence of prayer and the Spirit. Peter went up to pray on the housetop. He saw heaven opened and there came a vision that revealed the cleansing of the Gentiles. Then came the message of the men from Cornelius, a man who "prayed regularly" (Acts 10:2) and had heard from an angel: "Your prayers. . .have been received by God as an offering!" Then the voice of the Spirit was heard saying, "Go with them" (verse 20).

It is a praying Peter to whom the will of God is revealed and who is brought into contact with a praying and prepared company of hearers. In answer to all this prayer comes blessing beyond all expectation, and the Holy Spirit is poured out upon the Gentiles.

*Lord, my prayers never go unnoticed. Place within my
heart a desire for the gift of prayer. Speak to me in
quiet times. Teach me to hold fast to faith and wait
on You as Your Spirit rests in me. Amen.*

Stone Walls Give Way

But while Peter was in prison,
the church prayed very earnestly for him.

Acts 12:5

When we pray consistently, we will receive an entrance into God's will of which we would otherwise know nothing. We will receive blessing above all we ask or think. The teaching and power of the Holy Spirit are unalterably linked to prayer.

The power that the church's prayer has is shown not only as the apostles pray but also as the Christian community does. In Acts 12, Peter is in prison awaiting execution. The death of James had aroused the church to a sense of great danger; the thought of losing Peter, too, wakened all their energies. They went to prayer.

Prayer was effective; Peter was delivered. When he came to the house of Mary, he found "many were gathered for prayer" (verse 12). Double chains, soldiers, and the iron gate—all gave way before the power from heaven that prayer brought to his rescue. The power of the Roman Empire was nothing in the presence of the power that the church wielded in prayer.

Those Christians stood in close and living relationship with their Lord. They knew well that the words "I have been given all authority" (Matthew 28:18) and "Be sure of this: I am with you always" (verse 20) were absolutely true. They had faith in His promise to hear them whatever they asked. They prayed in the assurance that the powers of heaven not only could work on earth but also would work at the church's request on its behalf.

God, the prayer of a righteous person gains much. I have
been made righteous through relationship with Christ Jesus.
Help me to pray with assurance that the powers of heaven
are at work on earth and that Your will be done! Amen.

Linking with the King

So after more fasting and prayer, the men laid their
hands on them and sent them on their way.
ACTS 13:3

Acts names five men at Antioch who had dedicated themselves to ministering to the Lord with prayer and fasting. The Holy Spirit met them and gave them insight into God's plans. He called them to be fellow workers with Himself. There was a work to which He called Barnabas and Saul. The five men's part would be to send Barnabas and Saul with renewed fasting and prayer and to let them go, sent forth by the Holy Spirit.

God in heaven would not send His chosen servants without the cooperation of His church. People on earth were to have a partnership in the work of God. Prayer prepared them for this. The Holy Spirit gave authority to praying Christians to do His work and use His name. It was through prayer the Holy Spirit was given. Prayer is still the only secret of true church extension—prayer that is guided from heaven to find and send forth God-called and God-empowered men and women.

In answer to prayer, the Holy Spirit will indicate the people He has selected. In response to prayer that sets them apart under His guidance, He will give the honor of knowing that they are people sent forth by the Holy Spirit. Prayer links the King on the throne with the church at His footstool. The church, the human link, receives its divine strength from the power of the Holy Spirit who comes in answer to prayer.

Heavenly Father, create in me a deep desire for prayer
so that I may have a partnership in Your holy work on earth.
May my prayers prepare my path and provide me
with divine strength as I go forward. Amen.

Living Connection

Jesus Christ is the same yesterday, today, and forever.
HEBREWS 13:8

In the history of the church, two great truths stand out: Where there is much prayer, there will be much of the Spirit; where there is much of the Spirit, there will be ever-increasing prayer. When the Spirit is given in answer to prayer, it stimulates more prayer to prepare for a fuller revelation and communication of His divine power and grace. If prayer was the power by which the early church flourished and triumphed, is it not the one need of the church today?

Perhaps these should be considered axioms in our ministries:

1. Heaven is still as full of stores of spiritual blessing as it was then.
2. God still delights to give the Holy Spirit to those who ask Him.
3. Our life and work are still as dependent on the direct impartation of divine power as they were in Pentecostal times.
4. Prayer is still the appointed means for drawing down these heavenly blessings in power on ourselves and those around us.
5. God still seeks men and women who will, with all their other work of ministering, specially give themselves to persevering prayer.

God, everything depends on a direct impartation of Your divine power. May my time in prayer open my heart to a greater revelation of You so that I may draw close and earnestly give myself to persevering prayer. Amen.

Model of Intercession

They will pray day and night, continually.
Take no rest, all you who pray to the LORD.
ISAIAH 62:6

"Then, teaching them more about prayer, he [Jesus] used this story: 'Suppose you went to a friend's house at midnight, wanting to borrow three loaves of bread. You say to him, "A friend of mine has just arrived for a visit, and I have nothing for him to eat." And suppose he calls out from his bedroom, "Don't bother me. The door is locked for the night, and my family and I are all in bed. I can't help you." But I tell you this—though he won't do it for friendship's sake, if you keep knocking long enough, he will get up and give you whatever you need because of your shameless persistence' " (Luke 11:5–8).

Prayer is the one power on earth that commands the power of heaven. The early days of the church are a great object lesson of what prayer can do. Prayer can pull down the treasures of heaven onto earth.

Prayer is both indispensable and irresistible. Unknown blessing is stored up for us in heaven; that power will make us a blessing to men and enable us to do any work or face any danger. It is the one secret of success. It can defy all the power of the world and prepare men to conquer that world for Christ.

In all this prayer, there was little thought of personal need or happiness. Rather, there was desire to witness for Christ and bring Him and His salvation to others. It was the thought of God's kingdom and glory that possessed these disciples. We, too, must enlarge our hearts for the work in intercession.

Lord, prayer defies all the power of the world and gives
me the opportunity to conquer this world for Christ.
I pray You will fill my heart with greater passion
for the unlimited work of intercession. Amen.

The Urgent Need

"If you keep knocking long enough, he will get up and give you whatever you need because of your shameless persistence."

Luke 11:8

By intercession, our faith, love, and perseverance will be aroused. How may we become more successful in prayer? In the parable of the friend at midnight, Jesus teaches us that intercession for the needy calls forth our power of prevailing prayer. Intercession is the most perfect form of prayer; it is the prayer Christ ever lives to pray on His throne.

Intercession has its origin in urgent need. The friend came at midnight. He was hungry and could not buy bread. If we are to learn to pray as we should, we must open our eyes and hearts to the needs around us.

We hear of the billions of unreached people living in midnight darkness, perishing for lack of the bread of life. We hear of millions of nominal Christians, the majority almost as ignorant and indifferent as the heathen. We see millions in the church, not indifferent and yet knowing little of the power of a life fed by bread from heaven. If we believe what we profess, that God certainly will help in answer to prayer, this ought to make intercessors of us. It should motivate us to give our lives to prayer for those around us.

Let's face the need—Christless souls perishing of hunger, while there is bread enough and to spare! Our own neighbors and friends, people entrusted to us, die without hope! Christians around us live fruitless lives! Prayer is needed.

Lord, give me a heart like Yours for those who are lost, alone, and without a Savior. Show me how to give my life in prayer for those around me. . . that their hearts may be opened to know You. Amen.

Willing Love

*"A friend of mine has just arrived for a visit,
and I have nothing for him to eat."*

LUKE 11:6

The friend took his weary, hungry friend into his house and into his heart, too. He did not excuse himself by saying he had no bread. At midnight, he went out to seek food for him. He sacrificed his night's rest and his comfort to find the needed bread. "[Love] does not demand its own way" (1 Corinthians 13:5). It is the very nature of love to forget itself for the sake of others. It takes their needs and makes them its own. It finds real joy in living and dying for others as Christ did.

The love of a mother for her prodigal son makes her pray for him. When we have true love for others, we will have the spirit of intercession. It is possible to do much faithful and earnest work for others without true love for them. Just as a lawyer or a physician, out of a love of their profession and a high sense of faithfulness to duty, may become deeply involved with the needs of clients or patients without any special love for them, so servants of Christ may give themselves to their work with devotion and self-sacrificing enthusiasm without any strong, Christlike love. It is this lack of love that causes a lack of prayer. Love will compel us to prayer as that love and diligence are combined with the tender compassion of Christ.

*Lord, I pray for those who don't know You. I give myself
wholeheartedly to pray for their souls with devotion
and self-sacrificing enthusiasm. I earnestly pray
that they may come to know You! Amen.*

The Sense of Inadequacy

*"Don't bother me. The door is locked for the night,
and my family and I are all in bed. I can't help you."*

LUKE 11:7

We often speak of the power of love. In one sense, this is true,
and yet the truth has limitations. The strongest love may be
utterly inadequate. A mother might be willing to give her life
for her dying child but still not be able to save it. The host at
midnight was most willing to give his friend bread, but he had
none. It was this sense of inadequacy that sent him begging,
"A friend of mine has just arrived. . .and I have nothing for him
to eat" (Luke 11:6). This sense of inadequacy gives strength to
the life of intercession. "I have nothing for him to eat." As we
are aware of our inadequacies, intercession becomes the only
hope and refuge. I may have knowledge, a loving heart, and be
ready to give myself for those under my charge, but I cannot
give them the bread of heaven. With all my love and zeal, still "I
have nothing to set before him" (Luke 11:6 KJV).

Blessed are you if you have made "I have nothing" the motto
of your ministry. You think of the judgment day and the danger
of those without Christ and recognize a supernatural power is
needed to save people from sin. You feel utterly insufficient—
all you can do is to meet their natural need. "I have nothing"
motivates you to pray. Intercession appears to you as the only
thing in which your love can take refuge.

*Heavenly Father, intercession is my hope—the place I take
refuge. Help me to give up pleasures of things I would choose to
do today so that I may have time to intercede for others. Amen.*

Faith in Prayer

"Suppose you went to a friend's house at midnight,
wanting to borrow three loaves of bread."
LUKE 11:5

What the man in Luke 11 has not, another can supply. He has a rich friend nearby who will be both able and willing to give the bread. He is sure that if he only asks, he will receive. This faith makes him leave his home at midnight. If he himself has not the bread to give, he can ask another.

We need this simple, confident faith that God will give. Where that faith really exists, there will surely be no possibility of our not praying. In God's Word, we have everything that can motivate and strengthen such faith in us. The heaven our natural eye sees is one great ocean of sunshine, with its light and heat giving beauty and fruitfulness to earth. In the same manner, scripture shows us God's true heaven, which is filled with all spiritual blessings—divine light and love and life, heavenly joy and peace and power—all shining down upon us. It reveals to us our God waiting, even delighting, to bestow these blessings in answer to prayer.

Many promises and testimonies in scripture call and urge us to believe that prayer will be heard. What we cannot possibly do ourselves for those whom we want to help can be done and received by prayer. Surely there is no question as to our believing that prayer will be heard.

Father God, when I am empty and have nothing to give,
You are my source. You will provide for another what
I alone cannot. Help me to remain steadfast in prayer for those
who can benefit from the blessings You've given to me. Amen.

Persistency That Prevails

"Don't bother me. The door is locked for the night, and my family and I are all in bed. I can't help you."

LUKE 11:7

The faith of the host in Luke 11 meets a sudden and unexpected obstacle—the rich friend refuses to hear: "I can't help you." The loving heart had not counted on this disappointment and cannot accept it. The asker presses his threefold plea: Here is my needy friend, you have abundance, and I am your friend. Then he refuses to accept a denial. The love that opened his house at midnight and then left it to seek help must conquer.

Here is the central lesson of the parable: In our intercession, we may find that there is difficulty and delay in the answer. It may be as if God says, "I can't help you." It is not easy to hold fast our confidence that He will hear and then to continue to persevere in full assurance that we shall have what we ask. Even so, this is what God desires from us. He highly prizes our confidence in Him, which is essentially the highest honor the creature can render the Creator. He will, therefore, do anything to train us in the exercise of this trust in Him. Blessed is the man who is not staggered by God's delay or silence or apparent refusal but is strong in faith, giving glory to God. Such faith perseveres, importunately if need be, and cannot fail to inherit the blessing.

Lord, when it seems You have not responded to my prayer, I will hold tight to my confidence. I know You keep Your promises. Until You reply, I will keep praying because I have faith that You will provide what I have asked. Amen.

Certainty of a Rich Reward

*"But I tell you this—though he won't do it for friendship's sake,
if you keep knocking long enough, he will get up and give you
whatever you need because of your shameless persistence."*

Luke 11:8

Oh, that we might believe in the certainty of an abundant answer! Would that all who find it difficult to pray much would focus on the reward and, in faith, trust the divine assurance that their prayer cannot be in vain.

If we will only believe in God and His faithfulness, intercession will become the very first thing we do when we seek blessing for others. It will be the very last thing for which we cannot find time. It will become a thing of joy and hope because we recognize that we are sowing seed that will bring forth fruit a hundredfold. Disappointment is impossible: "But I tell you this—though he won't do it for friendship's sake, if you keep knocking long enough, he will get up and give you whatever you need because of your shameless persistence."

Time spent in prayer will yield more than time given to work. Only prayer gives work its worth and its success. Prayer opens the way for God Himself to do His work in and through us. Let our primary ministry as God's messengers be intercession; in it, we secure the presence and power of God.

"Suppose you went to a friend's house at midnight, wanting to borrow three loaves of bread" (Luke 11:5). This friend is none other than our God. In the darkness of midnight, in the greatest need, when we have to say of those we care for, "I have nothing for him to eat" (verse 6), let us remember that we have a rich Friend in heaven.

*God, thank You for Your faithfulness. Through intercession,
I desire to bless others. I have great joy and incredible hope
as I sow seeds of love and prayer into the lives of others. Amen.*

Start Now

"Commission Joshua and encourage and strengthen him."
Deuteronomy 3:28

Let us confess before God our lack of prayer. Lack of prayer is the proof of the lack of faith. It is the symptom of a life that is not spiritual—that is, still under the power of self and the flesh and the world. Let us by faith in the Lord Jesus give ourselves to be intercessors. May every sight of those needing help, every stirring of the spirit of compassion, every sense of our own inadequacy to bless, every difficulty in the way of our getting an answer all combine to urge us to do this one thing: with perseverance, cry to God who alone can and will help.

If we indeed feel that we have failed in a life of intercession until now, let us do our utmost to train a young generation of Christians to profit by our mistake and avoid it. Moses could not enter the land of Canaan, but there was one thing he could do. He could at God's bidding "commission Joshua and encourage and strengthen him." If it is too late for us to make good our failure, let us at least encourage those who come after us to enter into the good land, the blessed life of unceasing prayer.

Lord, when I fail to pray and intercede, my faith fails.
Forgive me for all the excuses I've made, and give me
the courage to step up to Your throne and begin again,
newly committed to intercession. Amen.

Because of His Persistence

*"If you keep knocking long enough, he will get up and give
you whatever you need because of your shameless persistence."*
LUKE 11:8

"One day Jesus told his disciples a story to show that they should
always pray and never give up. . . . Then the Lord said, 'Learn a
lesson from this unjust judge. Even he rendered a just decision
in the end. So don't you think God will surely give justice to
his chosen people who cry out to him day and night? Will he
keep putting them off? I tell you, he will grant justice to them
quickly!' " (Luke 18:1, 6–8).

Our Lord Jesus thought it so important for us to know the
need of perseverance in prayer that He gave two parables to teach
us. This aspect of prayer contains prayer's greatest difficulty and
its highest power. In prayer, we must expect difficulties which
can be conquered only by determined perseverance.

In the first parable, Jesus tells us that our Father is more
willing to give good things to those who ask than any earthly
father is to give his child bread. In the second, He assures us
that God longs to grant justice to His elect.

Urgent prayer is not needed because God must be made
willing. The need lies in ourselves. He uses the unwilling friend
and the unjust judge to teach that perseverance can overcome
every obstacle. The difficulty is in our incapacity to receive the
blessing. Because of our lack of spiritual preparedness, there is
a difficulty with God, too. His wisdom, His righteousness, even
His love dare not give us what would do us harm if we received
it too soon or too easily.

*Lord, thank You for this lesson and promise: determination
in prayer can overcome every hurdle. I open my heart to receive;
and as I pray, prepare my heart to receive Your wisdom,
Your righteousness, and Your answers. Amen.*

Strengthening Prayer Life

*"I tell you, you can pray for anything, and if you believe
that you've received it, it will be yours."*

MARK 11:24

The consequence of sin that makes it impossible for God to give at once is a barrier on God's side as well as ours. The attempt to break through the power of sin is what makes the striving and the conflict of prayer such a reality.

Throughout history, people have prayed with a sense that there were difficulties in the heavenly world to overcome. They pleaded with God for the removal of the unknown obstacles. In that persevering supplication, they were brought into a state of brokenness, of entire resignation to Him, and of faith. Then the hindrances in themselves and in heaven were both overcome. As God prevails over us, we prevail with God.

God has made us so that the more clearly we see the reasonableness of a demand, the more heartily we will surrender to it. One cause of our neglecting prayer is that there appears to be something arbitrary in the call to such continued prayer. This apparent difficulty is a divine necessity and is the source of unspeakable blessing.

Try to understand how the call to perseverance and the difficulty that it throws in our way is one of our greatest privileges. In the very difficulty and delay will the true blessedness of the heavenly life be found. There we learn how little we delight in fellowship with God and how little we have of living faith in Him. There we learn to trust Him fully and without reservation. There we truly come to know Him.

*Lord, strengthen my spirit with patience when the answers
don't come right away. Give me what I need to press on and
hold fast to Your promises. I believe what You have said
and know You will do it in Your perfect timing. Amen.*

Difficult Prayer

He prayed more fervently, and he was in such agony of spirit
that his sweat fell to the ground like great drops of blood.

LUKE 22:44

Have you ever noticed how much difficulties play a part in our life? They call forth our power as nothing else can. They strengthen character.

All nature has been so arranged by God that nothing is found without work and effort. Education is developing and disciplining the mind by new difficulties which the student must overcome. The moment a lesson has become easy, the student is advanced to one that is more difficult. It is in confronting and mastering difficulties that our highest accomplishments are found.

It is the same in our relationship with God. Imagine what the result would be if the child of God had only to kneel down, ask, get, and go away. Loss to the spiritual life would result. Through difficulties, we discover how little we have of God's Holy Spirit. There we learn our own weakness and yield to the Holy Spirit to pray in us. There we take our place in Christ Jesus and abide in Him as our only plea with the Father. There our own will and strength are crucified. There we rise in Christ to newness of life. Praise God for the need and the difficulty of persistent prayer as one of His choice means of grace.

Think what Jesus owed to the difficulties in His path. He persevered in prayer in Gethsemane, and the prince of this world with all his temptation was overcome.

Lord, I refuse to count my struggle as loss. The journey may
be difficult, but life's challenges increase my faith. My hope
rests in You alone. I will persevere in prayer and overcome
because You are the greater one living in me. Amen.

Persistence in Prayer

*"You can pray for anything, and if you believe
that you've received it, it will be yours."*

MARK 11:24

Persistence has various elements—the main ones are perseverance, determination, and intensity. It begins with the refusal to readily accept denial. This develops into a determination to persevere, to spare no time or trouble until an answer comes. This grows in intensity until the whole being is given to God in supplication. Boldness comes to lay hold of God's strength. At one time, persistence is quiet; at another, bold. At one point, it waits in patience, but at another, it claims at once what it desires. In whatever different shape, persistence always means and knows that God hears prayer: I must be heard.

Think of Abraham as he pleads for Sodom. Time after time, he renews his prayer until he has to say, "Please don't be angry, my Lord" (Genesis 18:30). He does not cease until he has learned how far he can go, has entered into God's mind, and has rested in God's will. For his sake, Lot was saved. "God had listened to Abraham's request and kept Lot safe" (Genesis 19:29).

Think of Jacob when he feared to meet Esau. The angel of the Lord met him and wrestled with him. When the angel saw that he did not prevail, he said, "Let me go." Jacob said, "I will not let you go" (Genesis 32:26). So the angel blessed him there. That boldness pleased God so much that a new name was given to Jacob—Israel, he who struggles with God—"because you have fought with God and with men and have won" (Genesis 32:28).

*Lord, when I pray, I will stand fast—with perseverance,
determination, and intensity. I refuse to give up.
I will not waver but will remain strong in my stance
until an answer comes from You. Amen.*

Pray and Prevail

The earnest prayer of a righteous person
has great power and produces wonderful results.

JAMES 5:16

When Israel had made the golden calf, Moses returned to the Lord and said, "Oh, what a terrible sin, these people have committed . . . . But now, if you will only forgive their sin—but if not, erase my name from the record you have written" (Exodus 32:31–32). That was persistence. Moses would rather have died than not have his people forgiven.

When God had heard him and said He would send His angel with the people, Moses went to God again. He would not be content until, in answer to his prayer, God Himself should go with them. God had said, "I will indeed do what you have asked" (Exodus 33:17). After that, in answer to Moses' prayer "Show me your glorious presence" (verse 18), God made His goodness pass before him. Then Moses at once began pleading, "O Lord. . .then please travel with us" (Exodus 34:9). "Moses remained there on the mountain with the LORD forty days and forty nights" (verse 28).

Moses was persistent with God and prevailed. He proves that the person who truly lives near to God shares in the same power of intercession that there is in Jesus.

James teaches us to pray for each other. "The earnest prayer of a righteous person has great power and produces wonderful results." Praise God! He still waits for us to seek Him. Faith in a prayer-hearing God will make a prayer-loving Christian.

Heavenly Father, I want to live my life wholly committed
to You. I desire Your presence at all times. I want to walk
with You each day. I want to hear Your voice and follow
Your direction. Teach me to pray. Amen.

The Mark of a Praying Christian

The earnest prayer of a righteous person has
great power and produces wonderful results.
JAMES 5:16

Remember the marks of the true intercessor: a sense of the need of those without Christ, a Christlike love, an awareness of personal inadequacy, faith in the power of prayer, courage to persevere in spite of refusal, and the assurance of an abundant reward. These are the qualities that change a Christian into an intercessor.

These are the elements that mark the Christian life with beauty and health. They fit a person for being a blessing in the world. These are the attitudes that call forth the heroic virtues of the life of faith.

Nothing shows more nobility of character than the spirit of enterprise and daring which battles major difficulties and conquers. So should we who are Christians be able to face the difficulties that we meet in prayer. As we "work" and "strive" in prayer, the renewed will asserts its royal right to claim what it will in the name of Christ.

We should fight our way through to the place where we can find liberty for the captive and salvation for the perishing. The blessings which the world needs must be called down from heaven in persevering, believing prayer.

Our work is often insignificant due to our lack of prayer. Let us change our method and make unceasing prayer be the proof that we look to God for everything and that we believe He hears us.

Lord Jesus, fill me with a deep passion for those who don't know
You. Instill in me a Christlike love, an awareness of personal
inadequacy, faith in the power of prayer, courage to persevere,
and the assurance of abundant reward. Amen.

The Life That Can Pray

*"I chose you. I appointed you to go and produce
lasting fruit, so that the Father will give you
whatever you ask for, using my name."*

JOHN 15:16

Our power in prayer depends upon our life. When our life is right, we will know how to pray in a way pleasing to God, and our prayer will be answered. "If you remain in me," our Lord says, "you may ask for anything you want, and it will be granted!" (John 15:7). According to James, it is the prayer of a righteous man that "has great power and produces wonderful results" (James 5:16).

In the parable of the vine, Jesus taught that the healthy, vigorous Christian may ask what he or she wishes and will receive it. He says, "If you stay joined to me and my words remain in you, you may ask any request you like, and it will be granted!" Again He says, "You didn't choose me. I chose you. I appointed you to go and produce lasting fruit, so that the Father will give you whatever you ask for, using my name."

What life must one lead to bear fruit? What must a person be in order to pray with results? What must one do to receive what he or she asks? The answer is simple. Live as a branch depending on the vine for strength. The source of power in prayer is the vine. If we are branches, abiding in Christ the Vine, He will supply the power. If we trust the vine, then we can ask what we wish and it will be granted.

Jesus, thank You for choosing me. I draw near to You today. Teach me to rely on You and to pray according to the will of the Father. I will bear fruit as I rely on You alone for strength. Amen.

Bearing Fruit

The earnest prayer of a righteous person
has great power and produces wonderful results.
JAMES 5:16

A branch is a growth of the vine, produced to bear fruit. It has only one purpose: that through it the vine may bear and ripen its fruit. As the vine lives to produce the sap that makes the grape, so the branch receives that sap and bears the grape. Its work is to serve the vine so that, through the branch, the vine may do its work.

The believer, the branch of Christ the heavenly Vine, is to live exclusively so Christ may bear fruit through him. A true Christian is to be devoted to the work of bearing fruit to the glory of God. With our life abiding in Him, and His words abiding and ruling in our heart, there will be grace to pray as we should and faith to receive whatever we ask.

The promises of our Lord's farewell discourse appear to us too large to be taken literally. We rationalize them to meet our human ideas of what we think they ought to be. We separate them from the life of devotion to Christ's service for which they were given. God's covenant is: Give all and take all. One who is willing to be nothing but a branch of Christ the Vine will receive liberty to claim Christ's riches in all their fullness and the wisdom and humility to use them properly.

Father God, I desire to live a life pleasing to You.
I remain dedicated to the work You have for me.
As Christ lives in me, may I bring glory to You. Amen.

Ask and It Will Be Done

Dear friends, if we don't feel guilty,
we can come to God with bold confidence.
1 JOHN 3:21

Think for a moment of the men of prayer in scripture and see in them lives that could pray in power. Abraham was an intercessor. What gave him such boldness? He knew that God had called him away from his home and people to walk with Him so that all nations might be blessed in him. He knew that he had obeyed and forsaken all for God. Implicit obedience, to the very sacrifice of his son, was the law of his life. He did what God asked, so he dared to trust God to do what he asked.

Moses was an intercessor. He, too, had forsaken all for God and lived at God's disposal. Often it is written of him that he did what the Lord commanded. No wonder he was very bold. His heart was right with God. He knew God would hear him.

We only pray the way we live. God longs to prove Himself the faithful God and mighty helper of His people. He waits to answer praying hearts wholly turned from the world and to Himself.

The branch that abides in Christ the heavenly Vine will bear fruit in the salvation of others. Such people may dare ask what they will—and it shall be done.

God, create in me a holy confidence. I choose to live obedient to Your will—no matter what You ask of me. I turn from the world to You and trust You will prove Yourself faithful all my days. Amen.

Pruning for Prayer

*"He prunes the branches that do bear
fruit so they will produce even more."*

JOHN 15:2

The more aware we become of our inability to pray in power,
the more we are helped to press on toward the secret of power
in prayer. Jesus said, "I am the true grapevine, and my Father
is the gardener" (John 15:1). We not only have Jesus Himself.
We have the Father, as the husbandman, watching over our
growth and fruit bearing. It is not left to our faith. God Himself
will see to it that the branch is what it should be. He will enable
us to bring forth just the fruit we were appointed to bear. "He
prunes the branches that do bear fruit so they will produce even
more." The Father seeks more fruit. More fruit is what the Father
Himself will provide.

Of all fruit-bearing plants, there is none that produces so
much wild wood as the vine. Every year, it must be pruned. It is
like this for the Christian. The branch that desires to abide in
Christ and bring forth fruit must yield itself to divine cleansing.

The gardener cuts away true, honest wood that the branch
has produced. It must be pruned because it draws away the
strength of the vine and hinders the flow of the juice to the
grape. The luxuriant growth of wood must be cast away so that
abundant life may be seen in the cluster.

There are things in you that sap away your interest and
strength. They must be pruned. Pruning results in a life that
can pray.

*Father, above all else, I desire to bear fruit. Bring forth
the harvest of all You have planted within my heart.
I embrace the pruning as You teach and strengthen
me in the way I should grow. Amen.*

Is Prayerlessness Sin?

"I will not remain with you any longer unless you destroy the things among you that were set apart for destruction."

JOSHUA 7:12

If we are to deal effectively with the lack of prayer, we must ask, "Is it sin?" Jesus is Savior from sin. When we experience sin, we can know the power that saves from sin. The life that can pray effectively is one that knows deliverance from the power of sin. But is prayerlessness sin?

Experiencing the presence of God is the great privilege of God's people and their power against the enemy. Throughout scripture, the central promise is that God is with us. The wholehearted person lives consciously in God's presence.

Defeat and failure are due to the loss of God's presence. This was true at Ai. God brought His people into Canaan with the promise of victory. With the defeat at Ai, Joshua knew that the cause must be the withdrawal of God's power. God had not fought for them. In the Christian life, defeat is a sign of the loss of God's presence. If we apply this to our failure in prayer, we see that it is because we are not in full fellowship with God.

The loss of God's presence is due to sin. Just as pain is nature's warning of a physical problem, defeat is God's voice telling us there is something wrong. He has given himself wholly to His people. He delights in being with them. He never withdraws Himself unless they compel Him to do so by sin.

Almighty God, create in me a clean heart. Purge all that is sinful and unholy. Speak to me and show me the things in my heart that need to be removed. Let nothing separate me from Your presence. Amen.

Revealed Sin

*"As for me, I will certainly not sin against the LORD
by ending my prayers for you. And I will continue
to teach you what is good and right."*

1 SAMUEL 12:23

We may think we know what sin is keeping us from prayer, but only God can truly reveal it. For example, after the defeat at Ai, He spoke to Joshua. "Israel has sinned and broken my covenant!" (Joshua 7:11). Israel had sinned. God Himself revealed it.

God must reveal to us that the lack of prayer is a greater sin than we have thought. It means we have little taste for fellowship with God. Our faith rests more on our own work than on the power of God. We are not ready to sacrifice ease for time with God.

When the pressure of work becomes the excuse for not finding time in His presence, there is no sense of absolute dependence upon God. There is no full surrender to Christ.

If we would yield to God's Spirit, all our excuses would fall away and we would admit that we had sinned. Samuel once said, "As for me, I will certainly not sin against the LORD by ending my prayers for you. And I will continue to teach you what is good and right." Ceasing from prayer is sin against God.

When God discloses sin, it must be confessed and cast out. If we have reason to think prayerlessness is the sin that is in "our camp," let us begin with personal and united confession. With God's help, let us put away and destroy the sin. Then we can know His presence and power.

*Father, I desire to depend wholly on You. I can do nothing
in my own strength. Bring me back to You when I fall
short, mistakenly thinking I can do things on my own.
My confidence rests in Your presence and power. Amen.*

God's Presence Restored

Restore to me the joy of your salvation.
PSALM 51:12

When sin is cast out, God's presence is restored. This truth is so simple. God's presence restored means victory secured. Then, if there is defeat, we are responsible for it. Sin somewhere is causing it. We need to discover the sin and repent. The moment the sin is put away, we may confidently expect God's presence.

God never speaks to His people of sin except with the purpose of saving them from it. The same light that shows the sin will show the way out of it. The same power that condemns will give the power to rise up and conquer.

God is speaking to us about this sin: "He was amazed to see that no one intervened to help the oppressed" (Isaiah 59:16). The God who says this will work the change in His children when they seek His face. He will make the shame of sin confessed a door of hope. Let us simply confess that we have sinned; we dare not sin any longer. In the matter of prayer, God does not demand impossibilities. He does not give us an impracticable ideal. He does not ask us to pray without giving the grace to enable us to do so. Believe Him. He will give the grace to do what He asks.

God, You have given me everything I need to succeed.
When sin enters, give me discernment to quickly recognize
it and repent. Allow me to experience Your grace and
forgiveness as I hunger for more of You. Amen.

The Secret of Effective Prayer

*"You can pray for anything, and if you believe
that you've received it, it will be yours."*

MARK 11:24

The more we enter into the mind of our Lord and think about prayer as He thinks, the more His words will grow in us. They will produce in us their fruit—a life corresponding to the truth they contain. Christ, the living Word of God, gives in His words a power that brings into existence what they say. This power accomplishes in us what He asks. It equips us for what He demands. View His teaching on prayer as a promise of what He, by His Holy Spirit, is going to build into your character.

The Lord gives us the five essential elements of prayer:

- the heart's desire
- the expression of that desire in prayer
- the faith that carries the prayer to God
- the acceptance of God's answer
- the experience of the desired blessing

Each Christian can say, "I want to ask and receive in faith the power to pray just in the way and just as much as my God expects of me." During the next few days, let us meditate on our Lord's words in the confidence that He will teach us how to pray for this blessing.

*Lord, fill me today with a deep desire to pray. I ask in faith
and believe I will receive the power to pray. You are the
living Word of God; and as I pray, Your words bring into
existence Your purpose and plans. Amen.*

Desire

"You can pray for anything, and if you believe
that you've received it, it will be yours."

MARK 11:24

Desire is the power that moves our whole world and directs the course of each person. Desire is the soul of prayer. The cause of insufficient prayer is often the lack of desire. Some may doubt this. They are sure they have earnestly desired what they ask. But if they judge whether their desire has been as wholehearted as God would have it, they may see that it was the lack of desire that caused the failure.

What is true of God is true of each of His blessings. "If you look for me wholeheartedly, you will find me" (Jeremiah 29:13).

We may have a strong desire for spiritual blessings. But alongside them are other desires occupying a large place in our interests. The spiritual desires are not all-absorbing. We are puzzled that our prayer is not heard. It is because God wants the whole heart. If there are desires which occupy more of our heart than He Himself, the desires that we are praying for cannot be granted.

We desire the gift of intercession, grace and power to pray as we should. Our hearts must give up other desires; we must give ourselves wholly to this one. By focusing on the blessedness of this grace, by believing with certainty that God will give it to us, desire may be strengthened. The first step will have been taken toward the possession of the desired blessing.

God, keep my heart from being divided between
Your desires for me and my own personal longings.
Please inhabit every space in my heart so that I may
pray and receive what is pleasing to You. Amen.

Express Your Desires

*"You can pray for anything, and if you believe
that you've received it, it will be yours."*
MARK 11:24

The desire of the heart must become the expression of the lips. The Lord Jesus more than once asked those who cried out to Him what they wanted. He wanted them to say what they desired. To declare it brought them into contact with Him and wakened their expectation. To pray is to enter into God's presence, to have distinct dealing with Him, to commit our need to Him, and to leave it there. In so doing, we become fully conscious of what we are seeking.

There are some who often carry strong desires in their heart but don't bring them to God in a clear expression of repeated prayer. There are others who go to the Word and its promises to strengthen their faith but do not pointedly ask God to fulfill them. Therefore their heart does not gain the assurance that the matter has been put into God's hands. Still others come in prayer with so many requests and desires that it is difficult for them to say what they really expect God to do.

If you want God to give you this gift of faithfulness in prayer and power to pray as you should, begin to pray about it. Declare it to yourself and to God.

*Father, I come to You with my deepest desires today.
I openly express my heart to You. I am confident
that as I place this situation in Your hands,
You will bring about the very best for me. Amen.*

Faith

*"You can pray for anything, and if you believe
that you've received it, it will be yours."*

MARK 11:24

It is only by faith that we receive Jesus Christ or live the Christian life. Faith also is the power of prayer. If we are to have our prayer for the grace of prayer answered, we must begin to pray in faith as never before.

Faith is the opposite of sight. They are contrary to each other. "We live by believing and not by seeing" (2 Corinthians 5:7). If heart and prayer are to be full of faith, we must withdraw from the visible. The person who seeks to enjoy life, who gives first place to the duties of daily life, is inconsistent with a strong faith.

"We don't look at the troubles we can see now." The negative action needs to be emphasized if the positive "rather, we fix our gaze on things that cannot be seen" (2 Corinthians 4:18) is to become natural to us. In praying, faith depends upon our living in the invisible world.

The reason for our lack of faith is our lack of knowledge of God and communion with Him. Jesus said to have faith in God when He spoke of removing mountains. When a soul knows God and allows the light of God to illuminate his life, unbelief will become impossible. All the mysteries connected with answers to prayer—however little we may be able to solve them intellectually—will be swallowed up in the assurance that this God is our God. He does answer prayer. He will delight to give the grace to pray that I am asking for.

*God, You have promised me faith that will move mountains.
I receive that faith today, Father. Fill my heart with a supernatural knowing so unbelief becomes impossible for me. Amen.*

Accept the Answer

"You can pray for anything, and if you believe
that you've recieved it, it will be yours."
MARK 11:24

Faith must accept the answer given by God in heaven before it is found on earth. This is the essence of believing prayer. Spiritual things can only be spiritually grasped. The spiritual blessing of God's answer to your prayer must be accepted in your spirit before you see it physically. Faith does this.

A person who not only seeks an answer but first seeks after the God who gives the answer receives the power to know that he has obtained what he has asked. If he knows that he has asked according to God's will, he believes that he has received.

There is nothing so heart-searching as this faith: "If you believe that you've received it, it will be yours." As we strive to believe and find we cannot, we are compelled to discover what hinders us. Blessed are those who, with their eyes on God alone, refuse to rest till they have believed what our Lord bids. Here is the place where faith prevails, and prevailing prayer is born out of human weakness. Here enters the real need for persevering prayer that will not rest or go away or give up till it knows it is heard and believes that it has received.

Father, work in my life according to Your will. I believe
and receive Your promise, even though I don't yet
know what You have planned for my future. Amen.

Experience the Blessing

*"You can pray for anything, and if you believe
that you've received it, it will be yours."*

MARK 11:24

Receiving from God in faith the answer with perfect assurance that it has been given is not necessarily the possession of the gift we have asked for. At times, there may be a long interval before we have it physically. In other cases, we may enjoy at once what we have received. When the interval is long, we have need of faith and patience. We need faith to rejoice in the assurance of the answer bestowed and to begin to act upon that answer, though for the present there is no visible proof of its presence.

We can apply this principle to our prayer for the power to be faithful intercessors. Hold fast to the divine assurance that as surely as we believe, we receive. Rejoice in the certainty of an answered prayer. The more we praise God for it, the sooner will the experience come. We may begin at once to pray for others in the confidence that grace will be given us to pray with more perseverance and more faith than we have done before.

If we do not find an immediate increase in our desire to pray, this must not discourage us. We have accepted a spiritual gift by faith; in that faith, we are to pray, doubting nothing. We may count upon the Holy Spirit to pray in us, even though it is with groanings which cannot find expression. In due time, we shall become conscious of His presence and power.

*God, give me a bold confidence as I pray. Impart a deep
understanding—to know Your grace empowers me to
pray ever more fervently. By the Holy Spirit, I pray. . .
even if I sometimes don't have the words. Amen.*

The Spirit's Presence

"And be sure of this: I am with you always,
even to the end of the age."

MATTHEW 28:20

When the Lord chose His twelve disciples, they were to accompany Him and He would "send them out to preach" (Mark 3:14). A life in fellowship with Him was to be their preparation for fulfilling the Great Commission.

When Christ spoke of His leaving them to go to the Father, their hearts were filled with great sorrow. The presence of Christ had become indispensable to them; they could not think of living without Him. To comfort them, Christ gave them the promise of the Holy Spirit, which would be a heavenly presence far more intimate than they had ever known.

Unbroken fellowship with Him was the power the disciples would need to preach and to testify of Him. When Christ gave them the Great Commission to go into all the world and preach the Gospel to every creature, He added the words: "And be sure of this: I am with you always, even to the end of the age."

This principle forever holds true for all His servants. Without the experience of His presence always abiding with us, our daily walk will have no power. The secret of our strength is in the Spirit of Jesus Christ being with us every moment, inspiring and directing and strengthening us. As you pray, be deeply convinced of Christ's words: "And be sure of this: I am with you always."

Lord, thank You for Your presence. I know You are always
with me. I pray You would continue to be my secret strength—
daily empowering, inspiring, and directing me in my faith walk.
I hear Your words, and I answer Your call. Amen.

The Omnipotence of Christ

"I have been given all authority in heaven and on earth."
MATTHEW 28:18

Before Christ gave His disciples their Great Commission, He first revealed Himself in His resurrected power as a partner with God Himself. It was the faith of this that enabled the disciples to undertake their mission with boldness.

Just think of what the disciples had learned of the power of Christ Jesus when He was here on earth. Yet that was little compared with the greater works that He would do in and through them. Christ provided the power to work even in the feeblest of His servants with the strength of the almighty God.

We, too, are to count literally upon the daily experience of being "strong in the Lord and his mighty power" (Ephesians 6:10). But remember, this power is never meant to be experienced as if it were our own. It is only as Jesus Christ as a living person dwells and works within our own heart and life that there can be power in our prayer and personal testimony. It was when Christ had said to Paul, "My power works best in weakness," that he could say what he had never learned to say before: "When I am weak, then I am strong" (2 Corinthians 12:9–10). It is the disciple of Christ who truly understands that all power has been entrusted to Christ and that we must receive that power from Him hour by hour.

Jesus, let my life be a continual song of praise
to You. As You live and dwell in me, I want others
to see You. I will share with others the amazing
things Your great love has done for me. Amen.

The Omnipresence of Christ

"I will be with you."
EXODUS 3:12

When Christ said to His disciples, "I have been given all authority in heaven and on earth," the promise immediately followed, "I am with you always" (Matthew 28:18, 20). The Omnipotent One is truly the Omnipresent One. The writer of Psalm 139 speaks of God's omnipresence as something beyond his comprehension: "Such knowledge is too wonderful for me, too great for me to understand!" (verse 6).

The revelation of God's omnipresence in the man Christ Jesus makes the mystery still deeper. The fact that we can experience this presence every moment is inexpressibly wonderful. And yet many of us find it difficult to understand all that Christ's presence implies and how, through prayer, it can become the practical experience of our daily life.

When Christ says "always," He means to give us the assurance that there should never be a moment in which that presence cannot be our experience. Yet it does not depend upon what we can effect but upon what He undertakes to do.

The omnipotent Christ is indeed the omnipresent Christ. His promise to us is: "I am with you always." Let your faith in Christ, the Omnipresent One, be in the quiet confidence that He will be with you every day and every moment. Meet Him in prayer and let His presence be your strength for service.

Christ, let my faith in You continue to grow. Give me a quiet confidence, that no matter what I face, I never have to face it alone. In Your presence I receive Your strength. Amen.

Christic: The Savior of the World

"He is indeed the Savior of the world."
JOHN 4:42

Omnipotence and omnipresence are what are called natural attributes of God. They have their true worth only when linked to and inspired by His moral attributes, holiness, and love. What lies at the root of these attributes is Jesus' divine glory as the Savior of the world and Redeemer of all men. It was because He humbled Himself and became obedient unto death that God so highly exalted Him. His share in the attributes of God was owing to the work He had done in His perfect obedience to the will of God. His finished redemption made salvation possible for humanity.

It is only when His servants demonstrate that they obey Him in all His commands that they can expect the fullness of His power and His presence to be with them. It is only when they are living witnesses to Christ's redemptive power to save and to keep from sin that they can experience His abiding presence. Then they will have the power to train others to the life of obedience that He asks.

The abiding presence of our Savior is promised to all who have accepted Him in the fullness of His redeeming power. What a privilege to meet in prayer with the One who has redeemed us. Our lives and words should proclaim to the world what a wonderful Savior He is.

Lord, You have saved me from sin, sickness, disease, and death. You have saved me from myself. Thank You for Your redeeming power. May I live a humble and obedient life that pleases You. Amen.

Christ Crucified

May I never boast about anything
except the cross of our Lord Jesus Christ.
GALATIANS 6:14

Christ's highest glory is His cross. It was in this that He glorified the Father and the Father glorified Him. In the fifth chapter of Revelation, Christ receives the worship of the ransomed and the angels and all creation. And it is as the Crucified One that His servants have learned to say: "May I never boast about anything except the cross of our Lord Jesus Christ." Is it not reasonable that Christ's highest glory should be our only glory, too?

It is the crucified Jesus who promises, "I am with you always" (Matthew 28:20). One reason why we may find it so difficult to expect and enjoy His abiding presence is because we do not glory in the cross. We have been crucified with Christ; our "old sinful selves were crucified with Christ" (Romans 6:6). This means we are crucified to the world and are free from its power. Consequently, we are to deny ourselves—to have the mind that was in Christ. He emptied Himself and took the form of a servant. He humbled Himself and became obedient even to death on the cross.

As we pray, it is the crucified Christ who comes to walk with us and in whose power we are to live the life that can say: "Christ crucified lives in me."

Lord, give me a greater revelation of Your death, burial,
and resurrection. I want to clearly see the gift You've
given. The more I know, the more I will desire to
see more of You and less of me. Amen.

Christ Glorified

"For the Lamb on the throne will be their Shepherd."
REVELATION 7:17

"And be sure of this: I am with you always" (Matthew 28:20). Who is it who speaks these words? We must take time to know Him well if we are to understand what we can expect from Him as He offers to be with us every day. Who is He? None other than the Lamb who had been slain in the midst of the throne! The Lamb in His deepest humiliation is enthroned in the glory of God. This is He who invites me to the closest fellowship with Himself.

It takes time in adoring worship and prayer to come under the full impression that Christ, before whom all heaven bows, is the one who offers to be my companion. He desires to lead me like a shepherd and to make me one of those who follow Him wherever He goes.

Read Revelation 5 until your heart is possessed by the thought that all heaven falls prostrate before Christ and the elders cast their crowns before the throne. The Lamb reigns amid the praises and the love of His ransomed ones and the praises of all creation. And if this is He who comes to me in my daily life and offers to walk with me, I cannot expect Him to abide with me unless my heart bows in surrender to a life of prayer, praise, and service.

*Lord, I accept the invitation to enter a close and personal
relationship with You. I surrender all to You. I gladly
bow my heart to a life of prayer, praise, and service.
I want to spend all my days with You. Amen.*

The Great Question

Jesus asked them, "Do you believe I can make you see?"
"Yes, Lord," they told him, "we do."
MATTHEW 9:28

"Jesus told her...'Anyone who believes in me will live, even after dying.... Do you believe this Martha?' 'Yes, Lord,' she told him." From what we have seen and heard of Christ Jesus, our heart is ready to say with Martha: "I have always believed you are the Messiah, the Son of God, the one who has come into the world from God" (John 11:25-27). But when it comes to believing Christ's promise to us of His abiding presence, we do not find it so easy to say, "I believe." Yet it is this faith that Christ desires to work within us.

We must understand clearly what the conditions are on which Christ offers to reveal to us the secret of His abiding presence. God will not force His blessings on us against our will. He seeks in every possible way to stir our desire and to help us to realize that He is able and willing to make His promises true. The resurrection of Christ from the dead is His great, all-prevailing evidence.

Now the great question is whether we are willing to take Him at His word and rest in the promise: "I am with you always" (Matthew 28:20). Christ's question to us is: "Do you believe?" Let us not rest until we have bowed before Him in prayer and said: "Yes, Lord, I do believe."

Lord, I take You at Your word and rest in Your promises today. Even though I did not see with my own eyes, I believe by faith that You were dead and rose again, to be forever alive. Thank You, Jesus. Amen.

Christt Revealing Himself

"Those who accept my commandments and obey them
are the ones who love me. And because they love me,
my Father will love them. And I will love them."

JOHN 14:21

Christ had promised the disciples that the Holy Spirit would come to reveal His presence with them. When the Spirit came, Christ showed Himself to them in a new, spiritual way. They would know Him far more intimately than they ever had while He was on earth.

The condition of this revelation of Himself is based on one word—*love*: "Those who accept my commandments and obey them are the ones who love me. And because they love me, my Father will love them. And I will love them." This is the meeting of divine and human love. The love with which Christ had loved them had taken possession of their hearts, and they would demonstrate that love by full and absolute obedience. The Father would see this, and Christ would respond to their loving hearts by revealing Himself to them.

But Christ doesn't just promise to reveal Himself to us. He also promises to dwell in the heart that loves Him. "My Father will love them, and we will come and make our home with each of them" (John 14:23). It is within the heart that is fully surrendered, showing itself in love and obedience, that the Father and the Son will take up residence. Christ's promise remains the same today: "And be sure of this: I am with you always." Oh, that everyone would believe and prayerfully claim the blessed promise: "I will love them and reveal myself to each of them" (verse 21).

Lord, let Your love take possession of my heart. As I
choose to obey You, I ask that You would reveal Yourself
to me more and more. I pray that I may know You
and love You more deeply each day. Amen.

Mary: The Morning Watch

"Mary!" Jesus said. She turned to him and cried out, "Rabboni!"
JOHN 20:16

Here we have the first manifestation of the risen Savior—to Mary Magdalene, the woman who loved Jesus so much.

Think of what the morning watch meant to Mary. Is it not proof of the intense longing of a love that would not rest until it had found the Lord? It meant a separation from all else in her longing to find Christ. It meant the struggle of fear against a faith that refused to let go its hold of Christ's wonderful promise: "Those who accept my commandments and obey them are the ones who love me. . . . And I will love them and reveal myself to each of them" (John 14:21).

That first morning watch, waiting in prayer for the risen Lord to reveal Himself, has been a joy to thousands of souls! With a burning love and strong hope, they wait for Jesus to manifest Himself as the Lord of glory. There they learn to dwell in the keeping of His abiding presence.

There is nothing that can prove a greater attraction to our Lord than the love that sacrifices everything and rests satisfied with nothing less than Himself. It is to such a love that Christ reveals Himself. He loved us and gave Himself for us. It is to our love that He speaks the words: "And be sure of this: I am with you always" (Matthew 28:20). It is love that accepts, rejoices, and lives in those words.

Thank You, Lord, for Your great sacrifice. Now that I have
known Your love, I never want to be separated from You.
You have written my name in the palm of Your hand.
You are forever mine, and I am Yours. Amen.

Emmaus: The Evening Prayer

As they sat down to eat, he took the bread.... Suddenly,
their eyes were opened, and they recognized him.
LUKE 24:30-31

Mary teaches us what the morning watch can mean for the revelation of Jesus to the soul. Emmaus reminds us of the place that the evening prayer has in preparing for the full manifestation of Christ in the soul.

When Jesus Himself approached the two disciples as they traveled, they did not recognize Him. But as the Lord spoke with them, their hearts began to burn within them. Yet they never thought that it might be Christ Himself. How often does Jesus come near with the purpose of manifesting Himself to us, and yet we don't see Him? When Jesus told the two disciples He must continue on His journey, their plea to spend the night caused Him to stay. We, too, should reserve time toward the end of the day when our whole heart prays with the urgency that constrains Him.

So what was it that led our Lord to reveal Himself to these two men? Nothing less than this: their intense devotion to their Lord. There may be much ignorance and unbelief, but if there is a burning desire that longs for Christ, He will make Himself known to us. In such intense devotion and constraining prayer, the Lord will open our eyes and we will know Him and enjoy the secret of His abiding presence.

Jesus, I desire to know You more. I want to recognize You in
every minute of my day. Open my eyes that I might see You
and rest in Your comforting presence. Amen.

The Disciples:
Their Divine Mission

Suddenly, Jesus was standing there among them!
"Peace be with you," he said.

John 20:19

The disciples had received Mary's message of Christ's resurrection. Late in the evening, the men from Emmaus told how He had been made known to them. Now their hearts were prepared for when Jesus stood in their midst and said, "Peace be with you," and showed them His hands and His feet. "They were filled with joy when they saw the Lord! Again he said, 'Peace be with you. As the Father has sent me, so I am sending you' " (John 20:20-21).

With Mary, He revealed Himself to her fervent love that could not rest without Him. With the men at Emmaus, it was their constraining prayer that received the revelation. Here He meets the willing servants whom He had trained for His service. He changes their fear into boldness to carry out the work the Father had entrusted to them.

For this divine work, they needed nothing less than divine power. He breathed upon them the resurrection life and fulfilled the promise He gave: "Since I live, you also will live" (John 14:19).

The word is spoken to us, too: "As the Father has sent me, so I am sending you.... Receive the Holy Spirit" (John 20:21-22). If our hearts are set on nothing less than the presence of the living Lord, we can be confident that it will be given to us. Jesus never sends His servants out without the promise of His abiding presence and His almighty power.

Lord, breathe on me Your resurrection power and fill me with divine revelation. Replace my fear with boldness to accomplish all the Father has given me to do. I receive Your Holy Spirit. Amen.

Thomas:
The Blessedness of Believing

"Blessed are those who believe without seeing me."
JOHN 20:29

Christ revealed Himself and allowed Thomas to touch His hands and His side. No wonder Thomas could find no words but those of holy adoration: "My Lord and my God!" (John 20:28). And yet Christ said: "You believe because you have seen me. Blessed are those who believe without seeing me."

True, living faith gives a far deeper and more intimate sense of Christ's divine nearness than even the joy that filled the heart of Thomas. Thomas had proved his intense devotion to Christ when he said, "Let's go, too—and die with Jesus" (John 11:16). To such a love, even when it was struggling with unbelief, Jesus Christ revealed Himself.

We, too, can experience the presence and power of Christ in a far deeper reality than Thomas did. To those who have not seen Jesus and yet believe, He has promised that He will reveal Himself and that the Father and He will come and dwell in them.

Yet we are often inclined to think of this full life of faith as something beyond our reach. Such a thought robs us of the power to believe. Take prayerful hold of Christ's word: "Blessed are those who believe without seeing me." This blessing only comes by the faith that receives the love and the presence of the living Lord.

Lord, today I take hold of Your Word: "Blessed are those who haven't seen me and believe anyway." I receive this blessing by faith, knowing I have experienced the presence of the living Lord. Amen.

Peter: The Greatness of Love

He said, "Lord, you know everything. You know
that I love you." Jesus said, "Then feed my sheep."

JOHN 21:17

In Christ's appearances after His death, it was to the intense devotion of the prepared heart that He revealed Himself. Now in the manifestation of Himself to Peter, it is again love that is the keynote.

We can easily understand why Christ asked the question three times, "Do you love me?" It was to remind Peter of the terrible self-confidence in which he had said: "No! . . . Even if I have to die with you, I will never deny you!" (Matthew 26:35). Peter was clearly in need of prayerful soul-searching so he could be sure that his love was true. He needed to understand that true love was the one thing needed for the full restoration to his place in the heart of Jesus.

God is love. Christ is the Son of His love. "I have loved you even as the Father has loved me" (John 15:9). Jesus asked that His disciples prove their love to Him by keeping His commandments and loving each other.

To everyone who longs to have Jesus reveal Himself, the essential requirement is love. Peter teaches us that such love is not in the power of man to offer. If the self-confident Peter could be changed so dramatically, we must believe that Christ will work that change in us, too. He will then reveal Himself to that loving heart in all the fullness of His precious word: "And be sure of this: I am with you always" (Matthew 28:20).

Lord, I am learning that without love, nothing works.
I choose today to demonstrate my love for You by
remaining obedient to all You have asked me to do.
Change my heart to forever reflect Your love. Amen.

John: Life from the Dead

"Don't be afraid! I am the First and the Last. I am the
living one. I died, but look—I am alive forever and ever!"
REVELATION 1:17–18

Sixty or more years after the resurrection, Christ revealed Himself
to the Beloved Disciple. John immediately fell as dead at His feet.
We learn from this that man's sinful nature cannot see the vision
of the divine glory and live. It needs the death of the natural life
in order for the life of God to enter in.

Christ then laid His hand on John and said, "Don't be afraid!
. . . I am the living one. I died, but look—I am alive forever and
ever!" He reminded John that He, too, had passed through death
so He could rise to the life and the glory of God. For the Master
Himself and for every disciple, there is only one way to the glory
of God—death to sin and self.

This lesson is a necessary one. Fellowship with Jesus—and
the experience of His living power—is not possible without the
sacrifice of all that there is in us of the world and its sin. The
disciples experienced this reality when Christ made this great
charge to them: Deny self, bear the cross, and follow Me.

Let us accept this lesson—through death to life. Since Christ's
death now works in us, we must yield ourselves in prayer to His
power and let Him live in and through us.

Lord, I turn my back on the sin of this world; I deny self
and follow You. Through Your sacrifice on the cross, I have
been blessed with eternal life. I surrender myself to You
and ask You to live in and through me today. Amen.

Paul: Christ Revealed in Him

God chose me and called me by his marvelous grace.
Then it pleased him to reveal his Son to me.

GALATIANS 1:15-16

Paul tells us that it pleased God to reveal His Son in him. He gives his testimony to the result of that revelation: "Christ lives in me" (Galatians 2:20). The chief mark of that life is that he is crucified with Christ. This enables him to say, "It is no longer I who live" (verse 20). In Christ, Paul had found the death of self. Just as the cross is the chief characteristic of Christ, so the life of Christ in Paul made him inseparably one with his crucified Lord. So completely was this the case that he could say: "May I never boast about anything except the cross of our Lord Jesus Christ. Because of that cross, my interest in this world has been crucified" (Galatians 6:14).

So if Christ actually lived in Paul so that he no longer lived, what became of his responsibility? His answer was clear: "I live in this earthly body by trusting in the Son of God, who loved me and gave himself for me" (Galatians 2:20). Paul's life was a life of faith in Christ who had loved him and had given Himself completely for him. Consequently, Christ had undertaken at all times to be the life of His willing disciple.

The indwelling Christ was the secret of his life of faith, his power in prayer, the one aim of all his life and work. Let us believe in the abiding presence of Christ as the sure gift to each one who trusts in Him fully.

Lord, thank You for the honor of having You live in me
and through me. Help me not to become distracted
by the shiny things of the world; instead help me to
focus completely on the life I have in You. Amen.

Why Could We Not?

*"But this kind of demon won't
leave except by prayer and fasting."*
MATTHEW 17:21

The disciples had often cast out demons. But here they had been powerless. They asked the Lord what the reason might be. His answer is very simple: "You don't have enough faith" (Matthew 17:20). How is it that we cannot live that life of unbroken fellowship with Christ which the scripture promises? Simply because of our unbelief. We do not realize that faith must accept and expect that God will, by His almighty power, fulfill every promise He has made. We do not live in that utter helplessness and dependence on God alone which is the very essence of faith. We are not strong in the faith, fully persuaded that what God has promised He is able and willing to perform.

But what is the reason this faith is so often lacking? "But this kind of demon won't leave except by prayer and fasting." To have a strong faith in God requires a life in close touch with Him by persistent prayer. We cannot call up faith at our bidding; it needs close communion with God through prayer. It needs the denial of self—the sacrifice of a worldly heart. Just as we need God to give us faith and power, He, too, needs our whole being to be utterly given up to Him. Prayer and fasting are essential to this.

*God, as I enter into a time of fasting, keep my mind
on You. When selfish desires tempt me, help me to
shut them out with a deeper focus and commitment
to You, to Your Word, and to prayer. Amen.*

The Power of Obedience

*"And the one who sent me is with me—he has not
deserted me. For I always do what pleases him."*

<small>JOHN 8:29</small>

In these words, Christ tells us what His life with the Father was.
At the same time, He reveals the law of all communion with
God—simple obedience.

In John 14, He says three times: "If you love me, obey my
commandments" (verses 15, 21, 23); also in chapter 15: "When you
obey my commandments, you remain in my love, just as I obey
my Father's and remain in his love. . . . You are my friends if you
do what I command" (verses 10, 14). Obedience is the proof and
the exercise of the love of God in our hearts. It comes from love
and leads to love. It assures us that we are abiding in the love of
Christ. It seals our claim to be called the friends of Christ. So it
is not only a proof of love but of faith, too. It assures us that we
"will receive from him whatever we ask because we obey him and
do the things that please him" (1 John 3:22).

Obedience enables us to abide in His love and gives us the
full experience of His unbroken presence. It is to the obedient
that the word comes, "And be sure of this: I am with you always"
(Matthew 28:20), and to whom all the fullness of its meaning
will be revealed.

*Lord, I want to obey. As I obey, my heart will be opened
to clearly hear You and walk closely with You. I desire
to live in Your love and to experience Your unbroken
presence. Reveal Yourself to me. Amen.*

The Power of Intercession

*"Then we apostles can spend our time
in prayer and teaching the word."*

ACTS 6:4

In his travels throughout Asia, Dr. Mott was moved by the need for united prayer in the missionary endeavor. He writes: "There is no better way to serve the deepest interest of the church than by multiplying the number of real intercessors and by focusing their prayers on those situations which demand the almighty working of the Spirit of God. Far more important than any service we can give to missions is that of helping to release the superhuman energy of prayer.

"Immeasurably more important than any other work is the linking of all we do to the fountain of divine life and energy. The Christian world not only has a right to expect mission leaders to set forth the facts and methods of the work, but also a larger discovery of superhuman resources and spiritual power."

And where is there a greater need of focusing the united intercession of Christians than on the great army of missionaries? They tell of their need for the presence and the power of God's Spirit in their life and work. They long for the experience of the abiding presence and power of Christ every day. They need it; they have a right to it. Shouldn't we become a part of that great army that pleads with God for the power which is so absolutely necessary for effective work?

*Heavenly Father, I pray for missionaries. Fill them with
Your presence and power. May Your Holy Spirit pour out
blessings on them. When they reach out with Your love,
give them supernatural power to touch the lives
of those who need You. Amen.*

The Power of Time

My times are in thy hand.
PSALM 31:15 KJV

"My time is in Your hand. It belongs to You. You alone have a right to command it. I yield it wholly and gladly to Your disposal." What mighty power time can exert if wholly given up to God!

Time is lord of all things. The history of the world is proof of how, slowly but surely, time has made man what he is today. All around us we see the proofs, such as the growth of a child to manhood. It is under the law of time and its inconceivable power that we spend our lives.

This is especially true in communion with God—all on the one condition: that we have sufficient time with God. Yet we often confess the weakness of our spiritual life and the inadequate results of our work. This is due to the failure to take time for daily communion with God.

What can be the cause of this sad confession? Nothing less than a lack of faith in the God-given assurance that time spent alone with Him will indeed bring into our lives the power to do His work. Through prayer, submit your timetable to the inspection of Christ and His Holy Spirit. A new life will be yours if you fully believe and put into daily practice the words, "My time is in Your hand."

God, I commit this time each day to You. Fill me with the power to do my work according to Your will and purpose. Divinely direct me and fill my mouth with Your words, all for Your glory. Amen.

The Power of Faith

"Anything is possible if a person believes."
MARK 9:23

Scripture teaches us that there is not one truth on which Christ insisted more frequently than the absolute necessity of faith and its unlimited possibilities. Experience has taught us that there is nothing in which we fall so short as the simple and absolute trust in God to literally fulfill in us all He has promised. A life in Christ's abiding presence must of necessity be a life of unceasing faith.

What are the marks of true faith? First of all, faith counts upon God to do all He has promised. It seeks nothing less than to claim every promise that God has made, in its largest and fullest meaning. It trusts the power of an almighty God to work wonders in the heart in which He dwells and rests in the hope of what He will do. In the pursuit of the power which such a life of faith can give, our soul must take God at His word and claim the fulfillment of His promises. We must then look to Him, even in utter darkness, to perform what He has spoken.

The life of faith to which the abiding presence will be granted must have complete mastery of our whole being. This faith will be able to claim and experience the words of the Master: "And be sure of this: I am with you always" (Matthew 28:20).

God, I desire an ever-increasing faith. No matter what I face, I believe You will do all You have promised. I trust You to perform miracles and work great wonders in my heart. Amen.

John's Missionary Message

We proclaim to you what we ourselves have actually
seen and heard so that you may have fellowship with us.
1 JOHN 1:3

This is the calling of the preacher of the Gospel. His message is nothing less than to proclaim that Christ has opened the way for us simple men to have living fellowship with the holy God. He is to preach this as a witness to the life that he himself experiences. In the power of that testimony, he is to prove its reality and show how sinful man on earth can indeed live in fellowship with the Father and the Son.

The message suggests to us that the very first duty of the minister is to maintain close communion with God. He must be conscious of the fact that his life and conversation are the proof that his preaching is true, so that his words will appeal with power to the heart.

It is this living testimony that will encourage and compel us to surrender ourselves to Christ. It is this intimate fellowship with Christ that is the secret of daily service and prayer. It has the power to inspire wholehearted devotion to His service. It is in this intimate and abiding fellowship with Christ that the promise "I am with you always" (Matthew 28:20) finds its meaning.

This is what all Christians need—an abiding fellowship with God that will divinely influence the workers and the converts with whom they come in contact.

God, I live to proclaim the message of Christ and live
my life as a witness before others. May my life be a
demonstration of how sinful people on earth can
indeed live in close fellowship with You. Amen.

Paul's Missionary Message

And this is the secret: Christ lives in you.
This gives you assurance of sharing his glory.
COLOSSIANS 1:27

In Paul's mind, the very substance of his message was the indwelling Christ. He spoke of the "riches of the glory of this mystery—Christ in you, the hope of glory" (Colossians 1:27 KJV). Though he had preached this gospel for so many years as a missionary, he still asked for prayer that he might make that secret known.

The complaint is often made in regard to our churches that, after a time, there appears to be no further growth and very little of the joy and power for bearing witness to Christ Jesus. The question comes whether the church at home is living in the experience of this indwelling Christ, so that the sons and daughters whom she sends out also know the secret. The answer is in Paul's missionary message which culminates in the words: "Christ. . .in you. . .assurance of sharing his glory."

Paul deeply felt the need for prayer to enable him to give this message faithfully. Is there not a call to all those who pray for our missionaries, and to our missionaries themselves, to obtain the power that leads Christians into the enjoyment of their rightful heritage? May the church at home also share in the blessing of this truth.

Lord, I want to continue growing in You. Help me to forever
be aware and reverent of the fact that You live and dwell
in me. I desire to share the wonder and amazing blessing
of having You reside within my heart. Amen.

The Missionary's Life

You yourselves are our witnesses—and so is God—that we were devout and honest and faultless toward all of you believers.

1 THESSALONIANS 2:10

Paul more than once appeals to what his converts had seen of his own life. So he says: "We can say with confidence and a clear conscience that we have lived with a God-given holiness and sincerity in all our dealings. We have depended on God's grace, not on our own human wisdom. That is how we have conducted ourselves before the world, and especially toward you" (2 Corinthians 1:12). Christ had taught His disciples as much by His life as by His teaching. Paul also sought to be a living witness to the truth of all that he had preached about Christ.

Paul appeals to the example of his own life throughout his writings. In Philippians 4:9, Paul writes: "Keep putting into practice all you learned and received from me—everything you heard from me and saw me doing. Then the God of peace will be with you." In 1 Timothy 1:14, 16: "Oh, how generous and gracious our Lord was! He filled me with the faith and love that come from Christ Jesus.... Then others will realize that they, too, can believe in him and receive eternal life."

Let us believe that when Paul said, "It is no longer I who live, but Christ lives in me" (Galatians 2:20), he spoke of an actual abiding of Christ in him. Christ was working in him to do all that was well pleasing to the Father. While in prayer, do not rest until you can say, "The Christ of Paul is my Christ. His empowerment is mine, too."

Lord, work in my heart. Fill me completely with Your love. May I make choices and decisions that daily show others that they, too, can spend eternity in Your heavenly presence. Amen.

The Holy Spirit

"He [the Holy Spirit] will bring me glory by
telling you whatever he receives from me."
John 16:14

When our Lord spoke the words to the disciples in Matthew 28:20, "And be sure of this: I am with you always," they did not at first understand or experience their full meaning. At Pentecost, they were filled with the Holy Spirit. It was then that the Spirit brought down into their hearts the new life of Christ's abiding presence.

All our attempts to claim to live that life of continuous communion with Christ will be in vain unless we yield ourselves completely to the power and indwelling of the Holy Spirit. For the Spirit of God to show us what He can enable us to be, He demands complete possession of our whole being.

Christ meant the promise of His abiding presence to be accepted as absolute, divine truth. "And God has given us his Spirit as proof that we live in him and he in us" (1 John 4:13). But this truth can only be experienced when the Spirit of God is known and believed in and obeyed.

We need to understand that the Holy Spirit came as God to make known the Son in us. He claims absolute subjection and is willing to take possession of our whole being and will enable us to fulfill all that Christ asks of us.

Lord, I give my whole heart to the power of the Holy Spirit.
Show me all that You desire me to become. I give myself,
completely surrendered, to You. Amen.

Filled with the Spirit

Be filled with the Holy Spirit, singing psalms and
hymns and spiritual songs among yourselves,
and making music to the Lord in your hearts.
Ephesians 5:18-19

If we had the expression "filled with the Spirit" only in regard to the story of Pentecost, we might naturally think that it was something special and not meant for ordinary life. But our text teaches us that it is meant for every Christian and for everyday life.

To realize this more fully, think of what the Holy Spirit was in Christ Jesus and under what conditions He was, as man, filled with the Spirit. He received the Spirit when He was praying and yielded Himself as a sacrifice to God by going down into the sinner's baptism.

Full of the Holy Spirit, He was led to the forty days' fasting, sacrificing the needs of the body to be free for fellowship with the Father and for victory over Satan. He even refused, when He was famished, to listen to the temptation of Satan to use His power to make bread to supply His hunger. And so He was led by the Spirit all through life until He, by the Spirit, offered Himself without blemish unto God.

In Christ, the Spirit meant prayer, obedience, and sacrifice. It is only as we are led by the Spirit that we can abide in Christ Jesus, conquer the flesh and the world, and live the life with God in prayer and service.

Holy Spirit, fill me completely that I may live in power
and obedience, just as Christ lived. Only when I am
led by the Spirit can I truly conquer the flesh
and fulfill God's purpose. Amen.

The Christ Life

Christ lives in me.
GALATIANS 2:20

Christ's life was more than His teaching, more than His work, even more than His death. It was His life in the sight of God and man that gave value to what He said and did and suffered. It is this life that He gives to His people and enables them to live it out before men. It was the life in the new brotherhood of the Holy Spirit that made both Jews and Greeks feel that there was some superhuman power about Christ's disciples. They gave living proof of the truth that God's love had come down and taken possession of them. Everything depends upon the life with God in Christ being right.

It is the simplicity and intensity of our life in Christ Jesus, and of His life in us, that sustains us in our daily walk. It makes us conquerors over self and everything that could hinder the Christ life. Through prayer, it gives us the victory over the powers of evil.

The life in Christ must be everything to us because Christ Himself lives in us. When Jesus spoke the words "And be sure of this: I am with you always" (Matthew 28:20), He meant nothing less than this: "All day and every day, I am with you. I am the secret of your life, your joy, and your strength."

God, it is through Christ that I have been reconciled to You.
I was purchased at the highest cost, and You loved me
enough to pay it. I am no longer alone; Christ lives in me.
He is my hope today and for the future. Amen.

The Christlike Life

You must have the same attitude that Christ Jesus had.

PHILIPPIANS 2:5

What was the attitude that was in Christ Jesus? "Though he was God, he did not think of equality with God as something to cling to. Instead, he gave up his divine privileges; he took the humble position of a slave and was born as a human being. When he appeared in human form, he humbled himself in obedience to God and died a criminal's death on a cross" (Philippians 2:6–8). Self-emptying and self-sacrifice, obedience to God's will, and love to men, even unto the death on the cross—this was the character of Christ for which God so highly exalted Him. It is the character of Christ that we are to imitate. He was made in the likeness of men so we could be conformed into the likeness of God.

Self-effacement and self-sacrifice that God's will might be done and that man might be saved—this was the attitude of Christ. He lived only to please God and to bless men.

Don't say that this is an impossibility. What is impossible with men is possible with God. We are called to work out this salvation of a Christlike character with fear and trembling; for "God is working in you, giving you the desire and the power to do what pleases him" (verse 13). As we pray, let this be our one aim: to have the attitude that was in Christ Jesus.

*Lord, I sometimes have a bad attitude, and I respond
with my old ways of thinking. Help me to live and love
each day with a Christlike attitude. Give me the desire
to obey and do what pleases You instead of
thinking only of myself. Amen.*

Christ: The Nearness of God

Come close to God, and God will come close to you.
JAMES 4:8

It has been said that the holiness of God is the union of God's infinite distance from sinful man with God's infinite nearness in His redeeming grace. Faith must always seek to realize both the distance and the nearness.

In Christ, God has come very near to man. Now the command comes: If you want God to come still nearer, you must draw near to Him. The nearness of Christ Jesus expressed in the promise "And be sure of this: I am with you always" (Matthew 28:20) can only be experienced as we draw near to Him.

This means that at the beginning of each new day, we must yield ourselves to His holy presence. It means a voluntary, intentional, and wholehearted turning away from the world to wait on God to make Himself known to our souls. It means making time to allow Him to reveal Himself. It is impossible to expect the abiding presence of Christ with us through the day without the daily exercise of strong desire and childlike trust in His Word.

As you pray, let these words come to you with new meaning each morning: "Come close to God, and God will come close to you." Wait patiently, and He will speak in divine power: "I am with you always."

Heavenly Father, I want to live each day in Your holy presence. I turn away from this world and wait patiently for You to reveal Yourself to me. I will come close to You, and I trust You to draw close to me. Amen.

Love

*Jesus knew that his hour had come to leave this world and
return to his Father. He had loved his disciples during his
ministry on earth, and now he loved them to the very end.*

JOHN 13:1

These are the opening words of the talk that Jesus had with His
disciples in the last hours before He went to Gethsemane (John
13–17). They are the revelation of that divine love which was
manifested in His death on the cross.

He begins with the new commandment: "Love each other
in the same way I have loved you" (John 15:12). The new life in
Christ Jesus is to be the unfolding of God's love in Christ. He
continues: "I have loved you even as the Father has loved me.
Remain in my love. When you obey my commandments, you
remain in my love, just as I obey my Father's commandments
and remain in his love. . . . Love each other in the same way I
have loved you. There is no greater love than to lay down one's
life for one's friends" (John 15:9–13).

Can words make it plainer that the love with which the Father
loved the Son is to be in us? If by prayer we are to claim His daily
presence, it can only be as a relationship of infinite tender love
between Him and us. This love must be rooted in the faith of
God's love to Christ coming into our hearts and showing itself
in obedience to His commandments and in love to one another.

*God, sometimes I am overwhelmed by Your love. You know my
sins—past and present—yet You love me anyway. Your unwavering
love makes me want to please You more, Father. Amen.*

The Trial and Triumph of Faith

"Anything is possible if a person believes."
MARK 9:23

What a glorious promise: "Anything is possible if a person believes." Yet it is the greatness of this promise that constitutes the trial of faith. At first, we do not really believe its truth. But when we have grasped it, then comes the real trial in the thought: *Such a faith is utterly beyond my reach*. But what constitutes the trial of faith soon becomes its triumph.

When the father of the child heard Christ say, "Anything is possible if a person believes," he felt that this would only cast him into deeper despair. How could his faith be able to work the miracle? Yet we read that the father believed that Jesus not only had the power to heal his child but also the power to inspire him with the needed faith. The impression Christ generated upon him produced the second miracle: that he could have such great faith. And with tears, he cried, "I do believe, but help me overcome my unbelief!" (Mark 9:24). The very greatness of faith's trial was the greatness of faith's triumph.

Through our trials, we can experience the abiding presence of Him who speaks to us now: "I am with you always" (Matthew 28:20). Let us wait upon God in prayer until we can say in faith, "I do believe."

Lord, I want to trust, but sometimes the weight of a situation I am facing causes me to falter. Then I look to You, and You encourage me once again. Help my unbelief and restore me in the middle of trials and suffering. Amen.

Exceeding Abundantly

God. . .is able, through his mighty power at work within us,
to accomplish infinitely more than we might ask or think.
Ephesians 3:20

In the great prayer which Paul had just written, he had apparently reached the highest expression possible of the life to which God's mighty power could bring the believer. But Paul is not content. In this doxology, he rises still higher and lifts us up to give glory to God as "able to accomplish infinitely more than we might ask or think." Pause for a moment to consider what "infinitely more" means.

Think of the words "he has given us great and precious promises" (2 Peter 1:4). Think of "the incredible greatness of God's power for us who believe him. This is the same mighty power that raised Christ from the dead" (Ephesians 1:19-20). With these words, Paul hopes to lift our hearts to believe that God is able to do "infinitely more than we might ask or think." The power of God that works in us is nothing less than the exceeding power that raised Christ from the dead. This should cause us to think there is something that God will do in us that is beyond all our imagination.

As we worship Him in prayer, let us believe that the almighty God, who is working in our hearts, is able and willing to fulfill every one of His exceedingly great and precious promises.

Almighty God, Your work in me is endless and exceedingly
great. I cannot comprehend all that You want to do in my
life. I believe You will do more than I could ever hope
or imagine. Today I embrace Your purpose
and plan for me. Amen.

The Dispensation of the Spirit

*"How much more will your heavenly Father
give the Holy Spirit to those who ask him."*

LUKE 11:13

As he was meditating on prayer, the writer of a little book on prayer says: "I felt deeply that in this time of the working of the Holy Spirit, all we do in God's service is of little value unless it is inspired by the power of the Holy Spirit." This reminded me of the well-known text, "How much more will your heavenly Father give the Holy Spirit to those who ask him."

A priority for each of us every day should be asking the Father for the gift of the Holy Spirit to meet our daily needs. Without this, we cannot please God nor can we be of any real help to others. Our prayer that our lives fulfill God's purpose must have its origin in God Himself, the highest source of power. Water cannot rise higher than its source. If the Holy Spirit prays through us as human channels, our prayers will rise again to God who is their source. The prayers will be answered by God working in us. The Christian life of each one of us depends chiefly on the quality of our prayers and not on the quantity.

What material for deep meditation, for earnest prayer!

*Holy Spirit, I open my heart to You. I rest in the presence
of God, awaiting Your inspiration and purpose for me. I trust
You to meet my daily needs so that I may be a help to
others and live a life pleasing to God. Amen.*

The Fruit of the Spirit

But the Holy Spirit produces this kind of
fruit in our lives: love, joy, peace. . . .
GALATIANS 5:22

The first two lessons on prayer are: we must ask the Father to give us the Spirit anew every morning, and then ask the Spirit to teach us and help us. Here is a third lesson—commit to memory today's text.

Christians often think that they only need to ask God to teach them to pray and that He will do it at once. This is not always the case. What the Spirit does is strengthen our spiritual lives so we are able to pray better. When we ask Him to teach us, it is important that we first of all surrender ourselves to the working of the Spirit. This surrender consists in naming before Him the fruit of the Spirit, with the earnest prayer to be filled with this fruit. Think of the first three—love, joy, peace—the three chief characteristics of a strong faith life. Love: to God, to believers, and to all men. Joy: the proof of the provision for every need of courage and faith for all the work we have to do. Peace: the blessed state of undisturbed rest and security in which God can keep our hearts and minds.

In His last talk with the disciples, Christ used these words: "Remain in my love. . .so that you will be filled with my joy" (John 15:10–11). "I am leaving you with a gift—peace of mind and heart" (John 14:27).

God, today I choose to rest and remain in Your love—and to
become full of Your joy. With each of Your gifts, I experience
an overwhelming peace in my mind and heart. Amen.

Led by the Spirit

For all who are led by the Spirit of God are children of God.
ROMANS 8:14

Let us think about four other fruits of the Spirit: patience, kindness, goodness, gentleness. These all denote attributes of God. They will reach maturity in us as we pray for the working of the Holy Spirit.

Patience—In the Old Testament, God's patience was praised. All scripture bears witness to the patience God had for sinful man. "No, he is being patient for your sake. He does not want anyone to be destroyed, but wants everyone to repent" (2 Peter 3:9). This attribute of the Spirit will enable us to exercise divine patience with all sin and wrong so that sinners may be saved.

Kindness—We read wonderful things in the Psalms about God's kindness. "For his unfailing love toward those who fear him is as great as the height of the heavens above the earth" (Psalm 103:11). God can enable us to show this same mercy toward those around us.

Goodness—"Only God is truly good" (Luke 18:19). All goodness comes from God, and He gives to His children as each heart asks and desires. This goodness is manifested in sympathy and love to all in need.

Gentleness—It was chiefly in God's Son that the divine gentleness was shown. Jesus says: "Let me teach you, because I am humble and gentle" (Matthew 11:29). The Holy Spirit longs to impart gentleness to our hearts.

These four attributes of God may be brought to maturity in our hearts by the Holy Spirit so that we may be like Jesus.

God, I desire to live a life that pleases You. Develop in me patience, goodness, kindness, and gentleness. Lead me and teach me as I grow to maturity, becoming the person You created me to be, while demonstrating Your attributes to others. Amen.

The Spirit of Faithfulness

*We have the same kind of faith the psalmist had
when he said, "I believed in God, so I spoke."*

2 CORINTHIANS 4:13

Have you memorized Galatians 5:22–23 yet? If not, it is important
to do so. It will strengthen your desire to have the fruit of the
Spirit in you. Your expectation of God's blessing will be increased.
Let us consider the last two fruits of the Spirit—faithfulness and
self-control.

When the disciples asked the Lord: "Why couldn't we cast
out that demon?" His reply was: "This kind of demon won't leave
except by prayer and fasting" (Matthew 17:19, 21). They lacked
faithfulness. Even if they had prayed, they had not the enthusiasm
and self-sacrifice needed for prevailing prayer. Here we see faith
and self-control working together.

Faithfulness is a fruit of the Spirit. Such faithfulness believes
God's Word, clings to Him, and waits in perfect trust that His
power will accomplish all that He has promised.

Self-control enables us to use restraint, carefulness, and
unselfishness in our desires and in all our relationships. Our
goal should be: "We are instructed to turn from godless living
and sinful pleasures. We should live in this evil world with
wisdom, righteousness, and devotion to God" (Titus 2:12). We
should show self-control in all our dealings with the world and
its temptations, seek to be righteous in doing God's will, and live
in close communion with God Himself.

Memorize this text. Let the Holy Spirit lead you each day
to the Father so that the fruit of the Spirit will be seen in all your
actions.

*Heavenly Father, I desire to grow the fruit of the Spirit
in my life. I believe Your Word. I hold tight to You and
wait with a patient heart, trusting that Your power
will accomplish all You have promised. Amen.*

Worship God in the Spirit

We rely on what Christ Jesus has done for us.
We put no confidence in human effort.

Today let us worship God in the Spirit. We have come to the Father asking for the Holy Spirit. We have requested the guidance of the Holy Spirit. Now we begin to pray.

First, we pray to God the Father, thanking Him for His blessings. We acknowledge our entire dependence on Him and express our trust in His love and care for us. We wait before Him until we have the assurance of His presence.

Then we direct our prayer to the Lord Jesus and ask for grace to abide in Him always, for without Him, we can do nothing. We look to Him as our Lord, our preserver, our life, and give ourselves into His keeping.

Finally, we pray to the Holy Spirit. We ask Him to strengthen us so that what we have asked of the Father and the Son may happen. He is the dispenser of the power and gifts of the Father and of the Lord Jesus.

"We who worship by the Spirit of God are the ones who are truly circumcised. We rely on what Christ Jesus has done for us. We put no confidence in human effort." We have no power in ourselves to do good. We count on the Lord Jesus through the Holy Spirit to work in us. Take time to meditate on these things, asking God to grant His fruit in your life.

Father God, I have no ability to do good on my own; rather,
it is the Holy Spirit at work in me. I put my confidence
in You, trusting You to perfect everything that concerns
me as I stand secure in Your holy presence. Amen.

Intercession

Pray for each other.
JAMES 5:16

There is value in intercession. It is an indispensable part of prayer. It strengthens our love and faith in what God can do, and it brings blessing and salvation to others. Prayer should be mainly for others, not for ourselves alone. Begin by praying for those near and dear to us, those with whom we live, that we may be of help to them and not a hindrance.

Pray for your friends and all with whom you come into contact. Pray for all Christians, especially for ministers and those in responsible positions.

Pray for those who do not yet know the Lord as their Savior. Make a list of the names of those God has laid upon your heart and pray for their conversion. Christ needs you to bring to Him in prayer the souls of those around you. Pray, too, for all poor and neglected ones. Pray for mission work. Use a mission calendar with daily subjects of prayer.

Do you think this will take too much time? Just think what an inconceivable blessing it is to help others through your prayers. Look to the Holy Spirit for further guidance. If morning is not the best time for you, schedule another time later in the day. Cultivate the attitude: "I am saved to serve."

Holy Spirit, lead me in prayer on behalf of others.
Provide direction and guidance for those who find
it difficult to navigate life. Show them the way to
salvation, to deliverance, and to the peace that
is found in God alone. Amen.

Time

"Couldn't you watch with me even one hour?"
MATTHEW 26:40

Every minute spent in prayer is valuable. If ten minutes is all the time you can give, see what you can do in that time. Most people can spare more time. If you will only persevere from day to day, time will come of its own accord.

Is it possible that Christians can say that they cannot afford to spend a quarter or half an hour alone with God and His Word? When a friend comes to see us or we have to attend an important meeting or there is anything to our advantage or pleasure, we find time easily enough.

But God has a right to us and longs for us to spend time with Him, and we find no time for fellowship with Him. Even God's own servants are so occupied with their own work that they find little time for that which is all-important—waiting on God to receive power from on high.

Dear child of God, let us never say, "I have no time for God." Let the Holy Spirit teach us that the most important and profitable time of the whole day is the time we spend alone with God. Communion with God through His Word and prayer is as indispensable to us as the food we eat and the air we breathe. Whatever else is left undone, God has the first and foremost right to our time.

Holy Spirit, I recommit to spending time with the heavenly Father today. Instill in me a hunger for God's Word and an intimate relationship with Him through prayer. May time in His presence become of utmost importance in my life. Amen.

The Word of God

For the word of God is alive and powerful.
HEBREWS 4:12

I find it a great help to use God's Word in my prayers. If the Holy Spirit impresses a certain text upon my mind, I plead the promise. This habit increases our faith, reminds us of God's promises, and brings us into harmony with God's will. We learn to pray according to God's will and understand that we can only expect an answer when our prayers are in accordance with that will (1 John 5:14).

Prayer is like fire. Fire can only burn brightly if it is supplied with good fuel. That fuel is God's Word, which must be studied carefully and prayerfully. His Word must be taken into the heart and lived out in the life.

We are all familiar with the characteristics of a seed—a small grain in which the life power of a whole tree slumbers. If it is placed in the soil, it will grow and increase and become a large tree.

Each word or promise of God is a seed containing a divine life in it. If I carry it in my heart by faith, love it, and meditate on it, it will slowly, surely spring up and bring forth the fruit of righteousness.

The Holy Spirit uses both the Word and prayer. Prayer is the expression of our human need and desire. The Holy Spirit teaches us to use the Word as a guide to what God will do for us.

Holy Spirit, as I read the Bible, allow the words to become alive in me. As I meditate on the promises of God, help the seed of His Word grow in my life and become all that He promised. Amen.

The Name of Christ

*And whatever you do or say, do it as a representative of the
Lord Jesus, giving thanks through him to God the Father.*

COLOSSIANS 3:17

At the close of your prayer time, it is always well to add a request
for the Holy Spirit to "remind you of everything I [Jesus] have
told you" (John 14:26) all through the day. Then the prayers of
the morning will not be counteracted by the work of the day.

Read today's text once more, prayerfully. Have you ever
realized that it is a command? Is it the aim of your life to obey
it? This may be difficult, but it is not impossible or God would
not have asked it of us. God's Word has a wonderful power to
preserve the spirit of thanksgiving in our lives. When we get up
in the morning, let us thank God for the rest of the night in the
name of the Lord Jesus. In His name at night, thank Him for the
mercies of the day. The ordinary daily life full of most ordinary
duties will be lightened by the thought of what God has done for
us for Christ's sake. Each ordinary deed will lead to thankfulness
that He has given us the power to perform it.

At first, it may seem impossible to remember the Lord Jesus
in everything, yet the mere endeavor will strengthen us. The love
of Christ will enable us to live all day in His presence.

*Lord, I am thankful for Your grace and mercy, for Your
compassion and love for me. Throughout my day
remind me of the many things—big and small—that You
have done in my life, and I will give thanks. Amen.*

The Spirit Glorifies Christ

*"He will bring me glory by telling you
whatever he receives from me."*

John 16:14

To understand and experience the work of the Holy Spirit, you must try to grasp the relationship of the Holy Spirit to the Lord Jesus. Our Lord said that the Spirit would come as a Comforter to the disciples. The Spirit would reveal Him in their hearts. The disciples held on to that promise—they would not miss their Lord but have Him with them always. This made them pray earnestly for the Holy Spirit, for they longed to have Jesus with them always.

This is the meaning of our text—"He will bring me glory by telling you whatever he receives from me." Where there is an earnest desire for the glory of Jesus in the heart of the believer, the Holy Spirit will preserve the presence of Jesus in our hearts.

We must not weary ourselves with striving after God's presence. We must quietly endeavor to abide in fellowship with Christ, to love Him and keep His commandments, and to do everything in the name of Jesus. Then we will be able to count upon the secret but powerful working of the Spirit within us.

If our thoughts are always occupied with the Lord Jesus—His love, His joy, His peace—then the Holy Spirit will graciously bring the fruit of the Spirit to ripeness within us.

*Lord, I lift my heart and my thoughts to You. I rejoice
in Your unconditional love for me. I celebrate Your joy
and accept Your peace. May the Holy Spirit stir up Your
presence in me as I fellowship with You. Amen.*

Praying in the Spirit

Pray in the power of the Holy Spirit....
In this way, you will keep yourselves safe in God's love.
JUDE 20-21

Paul began the last section of the epistle to the Ephesians with the words "Be strong in the Lord and in his mighty power" (Ephesians 6:10). He speaks of the whole armor of God and closes by saying that this armor must be put on with prayer: "Pray in the Spirit at all times and on every occasion" (verse 18). Just as we need to be strong in the Lord and wear God's protective armor all day, so we need to live always praying in the Spirit.

The Holy Spirit will not come to us nor work within us just at certain times when we think we need His help. The Spirit comes to be our life companion. He wants us totally in His possession at all times; otherwise, He cannot do His work in us.

When this truth is grasped, we will realize that it is possible to live always praying in the power of the Spirit. The Spirit will keep us in a prayerful attitude and make us realize God's presence. Our prayer will be the continual exercise of fellowship with God and His great love. But as long as we regard the work of the Spirit as restricted to certain times and seasons, it will remain an unsolved mystery and a possible stone of offense.

Lord, as I put on the armor of God, I think about
the helmet of salvation that protects my mind as I strive
to have Christlike thoughts. I will wear Your protective
armor and stand strong in faith, praying always. Amen.

The Temple of God

For God's temple is holy, and you are that temple.
1 CORINTHIANS 3:17

From eternity, it was God's desire to create man as a dwelling place through which to show His glory. Because of man's sin, this plan seemed to be a failure. God sought a means of carrying out His plan in His people Israel. He would have a house in the midst of His people—first a tabernacle and then a temple—in which He could dwell. This was but a shadow of the true indwelling of God in redeemed mankind who would be His temple to eternity.

Since the Holy Spirit has been given, He has His dwelling in each heart that has been cleansed by the Spirit. The message comes to each believer however weak he may be: "Don't you realize that all of you together are the temple of God?" (1 Corinthians 3:16). How seldom this truth is experienced; and yet how true it is: "God's temple is holy, and you are that temple."

Paul testified: "Christ lives in me" (Galatians 2:20). This is the fullness of the Gospel which he preached: the riches of the glory of the mystery, Christ in you. This is what he prayed for so earnestly for believers: that God would strengthen them through His Spirit in the inner man. Yes, this is what our Lord Himself promised: "All who love me will do what I say. My Father will love them, and we will come and make our home with each of them" (John 14:23). Why is it that Christians are so slow to receive this wonder of God's grace?

Lord, I am honored that You would choose to live and dwell in me. Help me to present myself holy and pure in all that I do, that I may please You. May You always find my heart a welcoming place for Your presence. Amen.

The Fellowship of the Spirit

The fellowship of the Holy Spirit be with you all.

2 CORINTHIANS 13:14

In this verse, we have one of the main characteristics and activities of the Holy Spirit. It is through the Holy Spirit that the Father and Son are one and have fellowship with each other.

We also have fellowship with the Father and the Son through the Spirit. "Our fellowship is with the Father and with his Son, Jesus Christ" (1 John 1:3). "And we know he lives in us because the Spirit he gave us lives in us" (1 John 3:24). Through the Spirit, we know the fellowship of love with the Father and Son.

Through the Spirit, we, as God's children, have fellowship with each other. With the child of God, there should be no selfishness. We are members of one body. Through the Spirit, the unity of the body must be maintained. One reason that the Spirit does not work with greater power in the church is that the unity of the Spirit is not sought after. At Pentecost, after ten days spent in united prayer, the one hundred and twenty seemed melted together into one body. They received the Spirit in fellowship with each other.

We have fellowship when we meet at the communion table; we also have fellowship one with another in the trials of other members of the body. Our text reminds us: "The fellowship of the Holy Spirit be with you all."

In heaven, there is an eternal fellowship of love between Father and Son through the Spirit. Do we really long to be filled with the Spirit?

Heavenly Father, I pray that the fruit of the Spirit is evidenced by my fellowship with You. May my life be a testimony that shines bright as You help me to develop harmony in my relationships with both believers and unbelievers. Amen.

With the Whole Heart

"If you look for me wholeheartedly, you will find me."
JEREMIAH 29:13

It's often been said that if one seeks to perform any great work, he must do it with his whole heart and with all his might. In business, this is the secret of success. Above all in spiritual things, it is indispensable, especially in praying for the Holy Spirit.

Let me repeat that the Holy Spirit desires to have full possession of you. He can be satisfied with nothing less if He is to show His full power in your life.

Do you realize when you pray for the Holy Spirit that you are praying for the whole Godhead to take possession of you? Have your prayers had a wrong motive? If you were expecting that God would do something in your heart but in other things you would be free to do your own will, that would be a great mistake. The Holy Spirit must have full possession.

You may not feel a burning, urgent desire for the Holy Spirit to have full control, and you do not see any chance of its becoming true in your life. God knows about this inability of yours; He has ordained that the Holy Spirit will work within you all you need. What God demands of us, He will work within us. On our part, there must be earnest prayer each day and an acceptance of the Holy Spirit as our leader.

Child of God, the Holy Spirit longs to possess you wholly. Submit yourself in complete dependence on His promise.

*Lord, I seek You with my whole heart. I open my
heart fully and give You every compartment of my life.
I am completely dependent on You. I choose Your
will instead of my own today and every day. Amen.*

The Love of God in Our Hearts

For we know how dearly God loves us, because he has
given us the Holy Spirit to fill our hearts with his love.

ROMANS 5:5

God the Father fills our hearts with the Holy Spirit. Likewise, the
Holy Spirit fills our hearts with the love of God. As truly as God
has given us the Spirit, so truly is the love of God given by the
Spirit. Why do we so seldom experience this? Simply because of
our unbelief. It takes time to believe in the divine, mighty working
of the Holy Spirit. We need time to get away from the world and
its interests for our souls to rest in the light of God so that the
eternal love may take possession of our hearts. If we believe in
the infinite love of God and the divine power with which He takes
possession of the heart, then we will receive what we ask for—
the love of God filling our heart by the Holy Spirit. God desires
His children to love Him with all their heart and all their strength.
He knows that is impossible in our own strength. For that very
reason, He has given the Spirit to fill our hearts with His love.

If you long for this, draw near to God. Abide with Him in
quiet worship and adoration, and you will know the love of God
in Christ, which passes all knowledge.

God, I lift my heart and hands in adoration. You have shed
Your love abroad in my heart. I believe and receive that love.
I want to be the instrument You use so that others may
know and experience Your love, too. Amen.

Walk in the Spirit

Let the Holy Spirit guide your lives. . . .
Since we are living by the Spirit, let us follow the
Spirit's leading in every part of our lives.
GALATIANS 5:16, 25

The Christian in his daily walk must follow the leading of the Spirit. That will be the sign of a spiritual person who serves God in the Spirit and does not trust in his own abilities.

The Spirit is not needed just when we pray or just for our work for God's kingdom. God gives us His Spirit to be in us the whole day. We need Him most in the middle of our daily work because there the world has such power to lead us away from God. We need to ask the Father every morning for a fresh renewal of His Spirit. During the course of the day, let us remind ourselves that the Spirit is with us.

Paul says: "Now, just as you accepted Christ Jesus as your Lord, you must continue to follow him" (Colossians 2:6). Again: "Put ye on the Lord Jesus Christ" (Romans 13:14 KJV). Just as we put on a coat when we go out, so we must put on the Lord Jesus. We must show by our conduct that Christ lives in us and that we walk by the Spirit.

"Let the Holy Spirit guide your lives. Then you won't be doing what your sinful nature craves" (Galatians 5:16). If we are not under the guidance of the Holy Spirit, we will do things in our own strength. The Spirit is given to teach us that we may walk by the Spirit at all times.

God, I need You in every area of my life. Give me a
fresh outpouring of the Holy Spirit so that I may excel
in all that I do, living my life moment by moment
with a great desire to please You. Amen.

The Spirit Promised
to the Obedient

"If you love me, obey my commandments. And I will ask the Father, and he will give you another Advocate, who will never leave you."

JOHN 14:15-16

Christ would ascend to heaven and ask the Father to send the Comforter, the Holy Spirit. He would not do this only once, but it would become part of His intercessory work. "He lives forever to intercede with God on their behalf" (Hebrews 7:25).

The Lord tells us in John 14 on what conditions He will send the Spirit: If we love Him and keep His commandments, "I will ask the Father." The Holy Spirit is given to enable us to do the will of the Father. The conditions are reasonable and just. As we keep the commandments through the Spirit, the Spirit will be granted to us in fuller measure. Let us say to God that we will strive to keep His commands.

Do not listen to the whispers of Satan or give way to unbelief. Surrender yourself unreservedly to the Lord who has said: "If you love me, obey my commandments." Love will enable you to do it. Trust the Lord Jesus with childlike faith and give yourself completely to do His will—that is all that is necessary. Then the beauty of the divine agreement that He makes with us will become reality: "When you obey my commandments, you remain in my love" (John 15:10). The Father will send the Holy Spirit anew each day.

Lord, I know I miss the mark every day, but I want to be obedient and do Your will. Quicken my heart to hear Your voice, and help me refuse to go the way of a stranger. Help me to obey, Jesus. Amen.

The Spirit of Wisdom

I pray for you constantly, asking God. . .
to give you spiritual wisdom and insight
so that you might grow in your knowledge of God.
EPHESIANS 1:16–17

In the Word of God, we find a wonderful combination of the human and the divine. Anyone who has a good understanding of language can grasp the meaning of the words and the truths contained in them. But this is all that can be done in the power of human understanding.

There is a divine side in which the holy God expresses His deepest thoughts to us. We cannot understand them or comprehend them, for they must be spiritually discerned. Only through the Holy Spirit can the Christian apply the divine truth contained in God's Word. Much of our religion is ineffectual because people accept the truths of God's Word with their intellect and strive to put them into practice in their own strength. Even a young student in a theological seminary may accept the truths of God's Word as head knowledge, but the Word has little power in his heart to lead to a life of joy and peace in the Lord Jesus. Paul teaches us that when we read God's Word we should pray, "Father, give me spiritual wisdom and insight." As we do this each day, we will find that God's Word is living and powerful and will work in our hearts and lives.

Father, Your Word promises wisdom. Today I ask for
You to fill me with spiritual wisdom and understanding.
Help me to make sense of life's challenges and know what
You would have me to do in each case. Thank You. Amen.

The Spirit of Sanctification

God the Father...chose you long ago, and his Spirit has made you holy. As a result, you have obeyed him and have been cleansed by the blood of Jesus Christ.

1 PETER 1:2

In the New Testament, the word *holy* is attributed to the Holy Spirit. Christ set Himself apart for us that we might be holy. The great work of the Holy Spirit is to glorify Christ in us by purifying us.

Have you really understood this truth? The main object for which the Holy Spirit is given is to purify you! If you do not accept this truth, then the Holy Spirit cannot do His cleansing work. If you only want the Spirit to help you to be a little better and to pray a little more, you will not get very far. But when you understand that the Holy Spirit was given in order to impart God's holiness and will cleanse you completely, then you will begin to realize that the Holy Spirit dwells in your heart.

And what will be the result? You will want Him to be in complete control of your life each day.

Your whole life and conversation must be in the Spirit. Your prayer, your faith, your fellowship with the Father, and all your work in God's service must be completely under His control. As the Spirit of holiness, He is the Spirit of your purification.

This is a deep, eternal truth. But it will be of no consequence if we do not wait upon God to grant us the Spirit of divine wisdom and a vision of what God has intended for us—the Spirit of purification. Each morning pray: *Abba, Father, for this new day renew within me the gift of Your Holy Spirit. Amen.*

Father God, the Holy Spirit has done a great work in my heart and presented me holy and new. I am thankful for the chance to live in Your love, obedient to the purpose You have for me. Amen.

Rivers of Living Water

"Anyone who believes in me may come and drink!
For the Scriptures declare, 'Rivers of living
water will flow from his heart.' "

JOHN 7:38

Jesus, in His conversation with the Samaritan woman, said: "Those who drink the water I give will never be thirsty again. It becomes fresh, bubbling spring within them, giving them eternal life" (John 4:14). In John 7:38, the promise is even greater: rivers of living water flowing from Him, bringing life and blessing to others. John says that this refers to the Holy Spirit who would come when Christ had been glorified.

What do we need in order to experience the rivers of living water? Just one thing: the inner connection to Christ—the unreserved surrender to fellowship with Him. We have the firm assurance that His Spirit will work in us what we cannot do. We need a faith that rejoices in the divine power and love. We need a faith that depends on Him day by day to grant us grace that living water may flow out from us. If the water from a reservoir is to flow into a house all day, one thing is necessary: The connection must be perfect. Then the water passes through the pipe of its own accord. So the connection between us and Christ must be uninterrupted. Our faith must accept Christ and depend on Him to sustain the new life.

Jesus, thank You for the power of the Holy Spirit. I rejoice in the
eternal life that I have through You. I have faith and confidence
in the work You are doing each day of my life. Amen.

Joy in God

*For the Kingdom of God is not a matter of what
we eat or drink, but of living a life of goodness
and peace and joy in the Holy Spirit.*

ROMANS 14:17

A Christian man said to me shortly after his conversion: "I always thought that if I became religious, it would be impossible for me to do my worldly business. The two things seemed so contrary. I seemed to be a man trying to dig a vineyard with a bag of sand on his shoulders. But when I found the Lord, I was so filled with joy that I could do my work cheerfully from morning till night. The bag of sand was gone; the joy of the Lord was my strength."

Many Christians do not understand that the joy of the Lord will keep them and enable them for their work. Read the scriptures and see how the kingdom of God is pure joy and peace through the Holy Spirit. God will "fill you completely with joy and peace because you trust in him. . .through the power of the Holy Spirit" (Romans 15:13).

Then try to realize that the Holy Spirit will give this joy and peace of Christ in our hearts. It is wrong to think of the Holy Spirit as a matter of grief and self-reproach, of disappointment, of something too high and holy. The great gift of the Father is meant to keep us in the joy and peace of Christ.

Listen attentively to the voice of the Spirit each day as He points to Jesus Christ, who offers you His wonderful fruit: love, joy, peace.

*Lord, Your joy is my strength. Help me to choose joy no matter
what obstacles I might face. When I am tempted to complain,
remind me of the joy that You have made available to me. Amen.*

All the Day—Every Day

I will praise you every day.
PSALM 145:2

It is a step forward in the Christian life when you seek to have fellowship with God in His Word each day without fail. Perseverance will be crowned with success if you are really sincere. The experience may be somewhat as follows:

When you wake up in the morning, God will be your first thought. Set apart a time for prayer and resolve to give God time to hear requests and to reveal Himself. You may share all your desires with God and expect an answer.

Later on in the day, even if only for a few minutes, take time to keep up the fellowship with God. And again in the evening, take time to reflect on the day's work and, with confession of sin, receive the assurance of forgiveness. Then commit yourself anew to God and His service.

Gradually, you will get an insight into what is lacking in life and will be ready for uninterrupted fellowship with God through the Holy Spirit. You will gain the assurance through faith that the Holy Spirit, the Lord Jesus, and the Father Himself will give His presence and help all through the day.

Remember that you only need to live life one day at a time. You don't have to worry about tomorrow, but rest in the assurance that He who has led you today will be even closer tomorrow.

God, when I wake up, let my thoughts immediately go to You.
As I go about my day, direct my thoughts to Your goodness,
Your mercy, and Your love. May I remain connected
to You every minute of the day, Father. Amen.

The Spirit and the Cross

For by the power of the eternal Spirit, Christ offered
himself to God as a perfect sacrifice for our sins.
HEBREWS 9:14

The connection between the cross and the Spirit is inconceivably close and meaningful. The Spirit brought Christ to the cross and enabled Him to die there. The cross gave Christ the right to bring down the Holy Spirit on earth because there He made reconciliation for sin. The cross gave Christ the right and the power to grant us the power of the Spirit because on it He set us free from the power of sin.

Christ could not have attained to the heavenly life or poured out the Holy Spirit if He had not first died to sin, to the world, and to His own life. He died to sin that He might live to God. And that is the way the Holy Spirit brings the cross into our hearts. It is only as we have been crucified with Christ that we can receive the full power of the Spirit. When we do not realize how necessary it is to die to all earthly things, the Spirit cannot gain full possession of us.

If we as Christians rely only on our human understanding, we cannot understand or experience that the fellowship of the Spirit is a fellowship of the cross. Wait on God to teach you divine truths through the Spirit.

Lord, alone I am unable to understand the cross
and what it means. But by the Spirit, I know You can
teach me how to bring the cross into my heart and
receive all that You sacrificed for me. Amen.

The Spirit and the Blood

So we have these three witnesses—the Spirit,
the water, and the blood—and all three agree.

1 JOHN 5:7–8

Baptism by water is an external sign of inner renewing and purifying through regeneration. The Spirit and the blood are spiritual expressions, working together in regeneration: the blood for the forgiveness of sins, the Spirit for the renewal of the whole nature.

There is spiritual oneness in the Spirit and the blood. Through the blood, we obtain the Spirit, as through the blood we are redeemed and purified to receive the Spirit. Only through the blood can we pray with confidence to receive the Spirit.

There may be some sin in your life of which you are hardly conscious but which grieves the Spirit and drives Him away. The only way to avoid this is to believe that "the blood of Jesus, his Son, cleanses us from all sin" (1 John 1:7). Your only right to approach God is through the blood of the Lamb. Come with every sin, known or unknown, and plead the blood of Christ as your only claim to forgiveness.

But do not be content with just the forgiveness of sins. Accept the fullness of the Spirit that comes by the blood of Christ. Do not for a moment doubt that you have a right through the blood to the fullness of the Spirit.

As one who has been redeemed by the blood, give yourself to God as His purchased possession—a vessel ready for Him to use, a dwelling place of the Holy Spirit.

Heavenly Father, You have purchased my salvation at
a great price. I give my life to You in service and faith.
Thank You for the blood of Jesus that cleansed me
from all sin and provided restoration of my soul. Amen.

The Spirit in Preacher
and Hearer

*For when we brought you the Good News, it was
not only with words but also with power.... So you
received the message with joy from the Holy Spirit.*

1 THESSALONIANS 1:5–6

Paul more than once reminds his converts that the chief characteristic of his preaching was the supernatural power of the Holy Spirit. This is one of the most important lessons in the spiritual life. We as hearers are accustomed to listening attentively to the sermon to see what it has to teach us. But we may forget that the blessing of our churchgoing depends on two things. First, it depends on the prayer for the preacher that the Holy Spirit will be powerful and prayer for ourselves that we may receive the word not from people but as God's Word, which "continues to work in you who believe" (1 Thessalonians 2:13). How often there is no manifestation of the Spirit when both the speaking and the hearing are mainly the work of human understanding or feeling.

We should pray earnestly that God will reveal to both minister and people "spiritual wisdom and insight" (Ephesians 1:17) that we may discover what place the Holy Spirit really should have in our lives. As God gives us wisdom, we will understand what Christ meant when He said: "Do not leave Jerusalem until the Father sends you the gift he promised.... But you will receive power when the Holy Spirit comes upon you. And you will be my witnesses, telling people about me everywhere...to the ends of the earth" (Acts 1:4, 8).

*Lord, as I go to church, I pray the Holy Spirit has influence
over the words and heart of the preacher. I pray for our
congregation, that our hearts would be open to receive
what the Spirit is sharing from God's Word. Amen.*

The Full Gospel

"You must repent of your sins and turn to God,
and be baptized in the name of Jesus Christ. . . .
Then you will receive the gift of the Holy Spirit."

ACTS 2:38

When John the Baptist preached, "Repent of your sins and turn to God, for the Kingdom of Heaven is near" (Matthew 3:2), he also said: "Someone is coming soon who is greater than I am. . . . He will baptize you with the Holy Spirit and with fire" (Matthew 3:11). When Christ preached the Gospel of the kingdom, He said: "And I tell you the truth, some standing here right now will not die before they see the Son of Man coming in his Kingdom" (Matthew 16:28). This is what happened at the outpouring of the Holy Spirit.

Peter preached on the day of Pentecost the full Gospel of repentance, forgiveness of sins, and the gift of the Holy Spirit. This is indispensable in preaching the Gospel, for only then is it possible for a Christian to live in the will of God and to please Him in all things. The continuous joy of which Christ speaks can only be obtained through the power of the Holy Spirit.

How often only half the Gospel is preached—conversion and forgiveness of sins. The appropriation of the life of the Spirit is not mentioned. No wonder so many Christians fail to understand that they must depend each day on the Spirit.

Accept this truth for yourself. The daily enjoyment of the leading of God's Spirit is indispensable for a joyous life of faith. Ask the Father to grant you the gift of the Holy Spirit anew each day.

Father, pour out Your Spirit on me anew each day. I depend on the Holy Spirit to lead and guide me. Speak to my heart, that I may willingly follow the path You have laid out for me. Amen.

The Ministry of the Spirit

Clearly, you are a letter from Christ showing the result of our ministry among you. This "letter" is written not with pen and ink, but with the Spirit of the living God. It is carved not on tablets of stone, but on human hearts.

2 CORINTHIANS 3:3

The Corinthians' church was a "letter of recommendation" (2 Corinthians 3:2) for Paul, showing how much he had done for them. Although he claimed nothing for himself, God had enabled him as a "minister of the Spirit" to write in their hearts "with the Spirit of the living God."

What a wonderful example of the work of a minister for his people! A preacher prepared to be a minister of the Spirit, with power to write in the hearts of his people the name and the love of Christ. No wonder Paul speaks of how "all of us who have had that veil removed can see and reflect the glory of the Lord. And the Lord—who is the Spirit—makes us more and more like him as we are changed into his glorious image" (verse 18).

May God restore the ministry of the Gospel to its original power! If only ministers and church members would unite in the prayer that God, by the working of His Spirit, would give the ministry of the Spirit its right place. We need to pray that God will teach the people to believe that when Christ is preached to them, they are seeing as in a mirror the glory of the Lord and may be changed into the same image by the Spirit of the Lord!

God, I join my faith with others, trusting You will teach us to open our hearts and churches to the work of the Holy Spirit, giving Him freedom to move and minister as You direct. Amen.

The Spirit from Heaven

And now this Good News has been announced to you by those
who preached in the power of the Holy Spirit sent from heaven.
1 PETER 1:12

Christ has taught us to think of God as our own Father in heaven who is ready to give His blessings to His children on earth. Our Lord Himself was taken up into the glory of heaven, and we are told that we are seated with Him in the heavenly places in Christ. The Holy Spirit comes to us from heaven to fill our hearts with the light, the love, the joy, and the power of heaven.

Those who are truly filled with the Spirit have a heavenly life in themselves. They are in daily fellowship with the Father and with the Son and seek the things that are above. Their main characteristic is heavenly mindedness. They carry with them the marks of their eternal, heavenly destiny.

How can we cultivate this heavenly disposition? By allowing the Holy Spirit, sent from heaven, to do His heavenly work in our hearts and to bring to maturity in our lives the fruit of the Spirit. The Spirit will lift our hearts to daily fellowship with God in heaven. The Spirit makes the glorified Christ in heaven present in our hearts and teaches us to dwell in His presence.

Heavenly Father, I seek the things not of this earth
but of heaven above. May I forever be heavenly minded
with a clear focus on my eternal, heavenly destiny
as I navigate this life. Amen.

The Spirit and Prayer

"I tell you the truth, you will ask the Father directly,
and he will grant your request because you use my name."
JOHN 16:23

In Jesus' farewell discourse (John 13–17), He presented life in the Spirit in all its power and attractiveness. Through the Holy Spirit, God's children can go directly to the Father and ask God to bless the world. Seven times, we have the promise repeated: "You can ask for anything in my name, and I will do it" (John 14:13–14; 15:7, 16; 16:23–24, 26). Read these passages over so that you may come to understand how urgently and earnestly our Lord repeated the promise.

During the ten days before Pentecost, the disciples proved this. In response to their continuous united prayer, the heavens were opened. The Spirit of God descended to earth, filling them with His life. They received the power of the Spirit that they might impart it to thousands. That power is still the pledge of what God will do. If God's children will agree with one accord to wait for the promise of the Father each day, there is no limit to what God will do for them. Christian, remember that the Holy Spirit will dwell in you with divine power, enabling you to testify for Him. But it also means that you may unite with God's children to ask in prayer greater and more wonderful things than the heart can imagine.

Lord, I pray for a spirit of revival to fall on Your people. May we come together in one accord and wait for the promise of the divine power made available to us through the Holy Spirit. Amen.

With One Accord in Prayer

They all met together and were constantly united in prayer.
ACTS 1:14

Jesus gave the command to His disciples: "Go into all the world and preach the Good News to everyone" (Mark 16:15). He added the promise: "And be sure of this: I am with you always" (Matthew 28:20). This command and this promise were meant not only for the disciples but also for us.

Before His ascension, Christ gave His last command with a promise. The command was: "Do not leave Jerusalem until the Father sends you the gift he promised" (Acts 1:4). The promise was: "You will receive power when the Holy Spirit comes upon you. And you will be my witness, telling people about me everywhere. . .to the ends of the earth" (verse 8). This command and this promise are also meant for us. As irrevocable as the command to preach the Gospel is the command to wait for the Father to send what He promised—"When the Holy Spirit has come upon you, you will receive power."

For ten days, the disciples pleaded in one accord, and their prayer was answered. The church of our day has tried to carry out the first command to preach the Gospel, but it has often forgotten the second command to wait for the Father to send what He promised. The power of the first disciples lay in the fact that they, as one body, were prepared to forget themselves and to pray for the Holy Spirit.

Whatever you may have learned from reading this book, learn one more lesson: daily prayer in fellowship with God's children is indispensable if the Spirit is again to come in power. Pray for power.

*Lord, I ask that You direct my path and bring the right prayer
partners into my life. I believe You will bring those who share
the same passions and desires for relationship with You,
and for the body of Christ and for prayer. Amen.*

Pray at All Times

Pray in the Spirit at all times and on every occasion.
Stay alert and be persistent in your prayers for all
believers everywhere. And pray for me, too.
EPHESIANS 6:18-19

Pray at all times. Who can do this? How can we do it when we are surrounded by the cares of daily life? How can a mother love her child at all times? I can breathe and feel and hear at all times because all these are the functions of a healthy, natural life. If our spiritual life is healthy, under the power of the Holy Spirit, praying at all times will be natural.

Pray at all times. Does it refer to continual acts of prayer, in which we are to persevere until we receive an answer, or to the spirit of prayerfulness that should animate us all day? It includes both. Jesus gives us an example of this. We have to spend special times of prayer in private. We are also to walk all day in God's presence with our focus on heavenly things. Without set times of prayer, the spirit of prayer will be dull. Without the continual prayerfulness, the set times will not be effective.

Pray at all times. Does it refer to prayer for ourselves or for others? It refers to both, but too often we confine it to ourselves. The death of Christ brought Him to the place of everlasting intercession. Our death with Him to sin and self sets us free from selfishness and elevates us to the dignity of intercessor—one who can get life and blessing from God for others.

Lord, show me how to reach a place of everlasting
intercession. Give me a clear picture of what that
looks like. As I follow You, may my life become an
example of continual prayerfulness. Amen.

Becoming Educated

I urge you. . .to pray for all people. Ask God to help them;
intercede on their behalf, and give thanks for them.
Pray this way for. . .all who are in authority.
1 TIMOTHY 2:1–2

Pray without ceasing. How can we learn to do that? The best way of learning to do a thing—in fact, the only way—is to do it. Begin by setting apart some time every day, say ten or fifteen minutes, in which you say to God and to yourself that you come to Him now as intercessor for others. It can be in the morning, in the evening, or any other time. Do not worry if you cannot set aside the same time every day. Just see that you do it. Christ chose you and appointed you to pray for others.

If at first you do not feel any special urgency, faith, or power in your prayers, do not let that hinder you. Quietly tell the Lord Jesus of your weakness. Believe that the Holy Spirit is in you to teach you to pray. Be assured that, if you begin, God will help you. God cannot help you unless you begin and keep on.

Pray at all times. How do I know what to pray for? Once you begin to think of all the needs around you, you will soon find enough to pray for. But to help you, each day for the next few weeks, we will concentrate on subjects and hints for prayer. Use and reuse these ideas until you know more fully to follow the Spirit's leading and have learned, if need be, to make your own list of subjects. These days can be a time of becoming educated in this matter of praying at all times.

Lord, I sometimes feel inadequate praying for others,
yet I will pray. Give me the right words to express what is
needed for each person, as I bring them before You. Amen.

How to Pray

The Holy Spirit prays for us with groanings
that cannot be expressed in words.
ROMANS 8:26

If only topics for prayer were given, one might fall into the routine of mentioning names and things before God and prayer would become a burden. Therefore "how to pray" hints are included. They are meant to remind us of the spiritual nature of prayer and of the need for divine help. They will encourage our faith in the certainty that God, through the Spirit, will give us grace to pray and will also hear our prayer. It takes time to learn to pray with boldness and to dare to believe that you will be heard.

Take a few moments each day to listen to God's voice reminding you of how certainly even you will be heard. Listen to Him calling you to pray with faith in your Father and to claim and take the blessing you plead for. Let these words about how to pray enter your heart and thoughts at other times, too. The work of intercession is one of Christ's great works on earth, entrusted to Him because He gave Himself as a sacrifice to God for us. The work of intercession is the greatest work a Christian can do. Give yourself as a sacrifice to God for others, and intercession will become your glory and your joy, too.

Lord, I will drop everything right now and listen to Your
voice. I commit to rest in Your presence, leaving behind
my anxieties, worries, and concerns. I am content
to sit and embrace Your peace. Amen.

What to Pray

Pray for each other.
JAMES 5:16

Scripture calls us to pray for many things: for all Christians, for all men and women, for all in government, and for all who are in adversity. It tells us to pray for sending missionaries, for those in the ministry of the Gospel, for believers who have fallen into sin, for those in our own circle of friends. The church is now much larger than when the New Testament was written. The number of ministries and workers is much greater. The needs of the church and the world are so much better known that we must take time to see where prayer is needed and to what our heart is most drawn.

The scriptural calls to prayer demand a large heart, taking in all saints, all men and women, and all needs. An attempt will be made these next days to indicate what the chief subjects are that need prayer and that ought to interest every Christian.

It may be difficult to pray for such large spheres as are sometimes mentioned. Where one subject appears of more special interest or more urgent than another, spend some time day after day to pray about that. If you really give time to intercession and the spirit of believing intercession is cultivated, the object is accomplished. While the heart must be enlarged at times to take in all, the more pointed and definite our prayer can be, the better.

Holy Spirit, expand my heart. Give me the capacity to pray for many things. Help me not to feel overwhelmed but to see this as an opportunity. . .as a loving act of obedience to my heavenly Father's commands. Amen.

Answers to Prayer

"Do not leave. . .until the Father sends you the gift he promised."
ACTS 1:4

When we pray for all believers, or for missions in general, it is difficult to know when or how our prayer is answered, or whether our prayer had any part in bringing the answer. To remind us that God hears us, we should take note of what answers we look for and when they come. On the day of praying for all believers, take those in your congregation or in your prayer group and ask for a revival among them. In connection with missions, take some special location or missionary you are interested in and pray for blessing. Record definite requests with regard to individuals or special areas and look for the answers. Expect and look for God's answers so that you may praise Him.

When committing to persistent, meaningful prayer—prayer that expects answers—it may be helpful to have a small prayer group. You may meet for prayer once a month with some special topic introduced for every day. You may meet for a year or longer with the aim of strengthening each other in the grace of intercession. If you were to invite some of your believing friends to join for some special requests, along with printed topics for prayer or to unite in prayer for revival, some might join you in the great privilege of intercession who now stand idle because no one has invited them.

Lord, I join with others in faith. Help us to hear Your reply, even the faintest whispers. May we never be too focused on our list of needs that we fail to notice an answer to prayer. Amen.

God Is Sufficient

"My grace is all you need."
2 CORINTHIANS 12:9

Who is sufficient for real intercession? The more we study and try to practice the grace of intercession, the more we feel overwhelmed by its greatness and our weakness. Let that feeling lead you to hear "My grace is all you need," and to answer truthfully, "Our qualification comes from God" (2 Corinthians 3:5).

Take courage; you are called to take part in the intercession of Christ. The burden and the agony, the triumph and the victory are all His. Learn from Him; to know how to pray, yield to His Spirit in you. He gave Himself as a sacrifice to God for us that He might have the right and power of intercession. "He bore the sins of many and interceded for rebels" (Isaiah 53:12).

Let your faith rest boldly on His finished work. Let your heart identify with Him in His death and His life. Like Him, give yourself to God as a sacrifice for others. It is your highest calling, your true and full union with Him.

Come and give your whole heart and life to intercession, and you will know its blessedness and its power. God asks nothing less, the world needs nothing less, and Christ asks nothing less; let nothing less be what we offer to God.

God, I am encouraged today as I pray, recognizing
my only power and my only success come from You.
I take to heart that Your gracious favor belongs to me,
and that is all I really need. Amen.

The Power of the Holy Spirit

*I pray that. . .he will empower you
with inner strength through his Spirit.*
EPHESIANS 3:16

Pray for the full manifestation of the grace and energy of the Holy Spirit to remove all that is contrary to God's revealed will. Do this so that we do not grieve the Holy Spirit. Then He can work with mightier power in the church for the exaltation of Christ and for our blessing.

All prayer unites in the one request—the power of the Holy Spirit. Make it your prayer.

Pray as a child asks a father. "You fathers—if your children ask for a fish, do you give them a snake instead? . . . If you sinful people know how to give good gifts to your children, how much more will your heavenly Father give the Holy Spirit to those who ask him" (Luke 11:11, 13).

Ask as simply and trustfully as a child asks for food. You can do this because "God has sent the Spirit of his Son into our hearts, promoting us to call out, 'Abba, Father' " (Galatians 4:6). This Spirit is in you to give you childlike confidence. Have faith in the fact that He is praying in you. In that faith, ask for the power of the Holy Spirit everywhere. Mention places or groups where you especially desire it to be seen.

*Father, I pray for the full display of the grace and power
of the Holy Spirit to remove all that opposes Your will.
Have Your way in my home, in my community,
in my church, and in my country. Amen.*

The Spirit of Prayer

"I will pour out a spirit of grace and prayer."

ZECHARIAH 12:10

The evangelization of the world depends first of all upon a revival of prayer. It is needed more than personal witness or missionaries. Deep down at the bottom of our spiritless life is the need for the forgotten secret of persistent, worldwide prayer.

Every child of God has the Holy Spirit in him to pray. God waits to give you the Spirit in full measure.

Pray in the Spirit as Paul taught us: "Pray in the Spirit at all times and on every occasion" (Ephesians 6:18). Jude also wrote: "Pray in the power of the Holy Spirit" (Jude 20).

On His resurrection day, our Lord gave His disciples the Holy Spirit to enable them to wait for the full outpouring on the day of Pentecost. It is only as we acknowledge and yield to the power of the Spirit already in us that we can pray for His full manifestation.

Lord, I accept the authority of the Holy Spirit already residing within me. I submit to His purpose and desire. I open my heart to receive the full benefits of His power to do Your will. Amen.

Pray for All Saints

Pray in the Spirit at all times and on every occasion. Stay alert and be persistent in your prayers for all believers everywhere.
EPHESIANS 6:18

Every member of a body is interested in the welfare of the whole and exists to help and complete the others. Believers are one body and ought to pray, not so much for the welfare of their own church, but for all saints. This large, unselfish love is proof that Christ's Spirit and love are teaching us to pray. Pray first for all believers and then for those around you.

Pray in the love of the Spirit. Jesus said, "Your love for one another will prove to the world that you are my disciples" (John 13:35). He taught us that we are to have the unity that comes from love. "I pray that they will all be one. . .so that the world will believe you sent me" (John 17:21).

Paul taught us to pray from love. "Dear brothers and sisters, I urge you in the name of our Lord Jesus Christ to join in my struggle by praying to God for me. Do this because of your love for me, given to you by the Holy Spirit" (Romans 15:30). And Paul's teaching was reinforced by Peter. "Most important of all, continue to show deep love for each other" (1 Peter 4:8).

If we are to pray, we must love.

Lord, help me to have an unselfish love. And then show me how to model that kind of love in my prayers for others. I pray that my love will continue to grow—and will be a testimony of my relationship with You, Jesus. Amen.

The Spirit of Holiness

"Make them holy by your truth;
teach them your word, which is truth."

JOHN 17:17

God is the Holy One. His people are a holy people. He speaks: "I, the LORD, am holy, and I make you holy" (Leviticus 21:8). Christ prayed, "Make them pure and holy by teaching them your words of truth." Paul prayed, "[May the Lord] make your hearts strong, blameless, and holy as you stand before God" (1 Thessalonians 3:13), and "May the God of peace make you holy in every way" (1 Thessalonians 5:23).

Pray for all the believers—God's holy ones—throughout the church. Pray that the Spirit of holiness may rule them. Especially pray for new converts. Pray for the believers in your own neighborhood or congregation, especially for any you are interested in. Think of their special need, weakness, or sin and pray that God may make them holy.

Pray, trusting in God's omnipotence. The things that are impossible with men are possible with God. Often when we ask for great things, we think there is little likelihood of their happening. Prayer is not only wishing or asking, but believing and accepting. Be still before God and ask Him to allow you to know Him as the Almighty One and leave your requests with Him who does wonders.

God, make me holy as You are holy. Draw me close to You
and show me those things that need attention in my life.
Teach me how to become more like You. Amen.

Kept from the World

"Holy Father. . .protect them. . . . I'm not asking you to take them out of the world, but to keep them safe from the evil one."

JOHN 17:11, 15

Pray that God's people may be kept from the world. The night before He was crucified, Christ asked three things for His disciples: 1) that they might be kept and cared for as those who are not of the world; 2) that they might be purified; and 3) that they might be one in love. You cannot do better than to pray just as Jesus prayed. Ask that God's people may be kept separate from the world and the evil one. Pray that they, by the Holy Spirit, may live as those who are not of the world.

Pray with confidence before God. "Dear friends, if we don't feel guilty, we can come to God with bold confidence. And we will receive from him whatever we ask because we obey him and do the things that please him" (1 John 3:21–22).

Memorize that verse. Get the words into your heart. Join the ranks of those who, like John, draw near to God with an assured heart that does not condemn them. Learn to have confidence toward God. In the quiet confidence of an obedient child, pray for those believers who sin (1 John 5:16). Pray for all to be kept from the evil one. And say often, "What we ask, we receive, because we keep and do."

Father God, keep Your people from the evil of this world. May the power of the Holy Spirit infuse us with strength to live separately, refusing to participate in things contrary to Your Word. Amen.

The Spirit of Love in the Church

The Holy Spirit produces this kind of fruit in our lives: love.
GALATIANS 5:22

"I pray that they will all be one, just as you and I are one—as you are in me, Father, and I am in you...that the world will know that you sent me and that you love them as much as you love me.... Then your love for me will be in them, and I will be in them" (John 17:21–23, 26). Believers are one in Christ, as He is one with the Father. The love of God rests on them and can dwell in them. Pray that the power of the Holy Spirit will put this love in believers so that the world may see and know God's love in them. Pray consistently for this.

Pray as one of God's reminders: "I have posted watchmen on your walls; they will pray day and night, continually. Take no rest, all you who pray to the LORD" (Isaiah 62:6). Study these words until your whole soul is filled with the realization: *I am appointed as an intercessor.* Enter God's presence with that faith. Approach the world's need with this thought: *It is my job to intercede.* Meditate on the fact that the Holy Spirit will teach you how to pray and what to pray for. Let it be a constant awareness: *My great life work, like Christ's, is intercession. My purpose is to pray for believers and those who still do not know God.*

Father, I pray that the world may come to know You by our love. Help us to come together and love each other instead of struggling against one another because of our differences. Teach us to love like You do. Amen.

163

The Holy Spirit and Ministers

I urge you. . .to join in my struggle by praying to God for me.
ROMANS 15:30

Paul and Timothy emphasized their need for prayer as ministers of Christ. "You are helping us by praying for us" (2 Corinthians 1:11). There are a lot of ministers in Christ's church, and they need prayer. They would have a mighty ministry if they were all covered with the power of the Holy Spirit. Pray for this in earnest. Think of your own minister and ask for the Holy Spirit's power especially for him. Ask that ministers everywhere be filled with the Spirit. Plead for them the promise, "Stay here. . .until the Holy Spirit comes and fills you with power from heaven" (Luke 24:49). "When the Holy Spirit comes upon you" (Acts 1:8).

Pray in private. "Go away by yourself, shut the door behind you, and pray to your Father in private" (Matthew 6:6). Jesus "went up into the hills by himself to pray" (Matthew 14:23; see John 6:15).

Take time to be alone with God to intercede for His servants. Don't think that you have no influence or that your prayers don't count. Your prayer and your faith will make a difference. Go away by yourself and pray to God for His ministers.

*Lord, I take this time now to pray for Your ministers. May
they speak the truth in love. May they have wisdom
and discernment that come straight from You. May
they love Your people as You love them. Amen.*

Christian Workers

You are helping us by praying for us.
2 CORINTHIANS 1:11

There are multitudes of Christian workers ministering in connection with our churches and missions, our schools and colleges, our publishers and bookstores, our public service and government offices, young men and young women, children and youth, our worship in music, our military personnel, our hospitals and clinics, prisons, and our poor. Praise God for this! How much more they could accomplish if each were living in the fullness of the Holy Spirit! Pray for them; it makes you a partner in their work. You will praise God each time you hear of blessings anywhere.

Pray with definite requests. Jesus asked the blind beggar, "What do you want me to do for you?" (Luke 18:41). The Lord knew what the man wanted, and yet He asked him. Verbalizing our wish gives meaning to our transaction with God. It awakens faith and expectation.

Being definite in your requests also helps you to know what answer you are looking for. Ask those you are praying for what they need. If they have prayer letters, use them as guides. Intercession is not mere words and pious wishes. Its aim is to receive and bring down blessing through believing, persevering prayer.

*Lord, I partner in faith with the many Christian workers
ministering to others on Your behalf. Give them strength
when they are struggling, answers to the questions they seek,
and a desire to always respond in love. Amen.*

Mission Work

One day as these men were worshiping the Lord and fasting,
the Holy Spirit said, "Appoint Barnabas and Saul for the
special work to which I have called them."

ACTS 13:2

The evangelization of the world depends, first of all, upon a revival of prayer. The need for the forgotten secret of prevailing, worldwide prayer is greater than the need for missionaries.

Pray that our missions' work may all be done in this spirit: waiting on God, hearing the voice of the Spirit, and sending out men and women with fasting and prayer. Pray that in our churches our mission interests may be in the power of the Holy Spirit and of prayer. It is a Spirit-filled, praying church that will send out Spirit-filled missionaries, mighty in prayer.

Take time when you pray. The psalmist said, "I give myself unto prayer" (Psalm 109:4 KJV). The early church leaders agreed. "We apostles can spend our time in prayer" (Acts 6:4). Solomon in his God-given wisdom said, "Don't make rash promises.... Let your words be few" (Ecclesiastes 5:2).

Time is one of the main standards to measure value. The time we give is proof of the interest we feel. We need time with God—to know His presence and to wait for Him to make Himself known. We need time to consider and feel the needs we pray for. We need time to pray until we can believe that we have received.

God, I pray that my heart comes alive with a yearning to pray for
the lost to be found. Let Your very presence rest on Your people
and encourage us to pray like we've never prayed before. Amen.

Missionaries

*"You will receive power when the Holy Spirit
comes upon you. And you will be my witnesses,
telling people about me everywhere."*

ACTS 1:8

Missionaries today need an outpouring of God's Spirit in their
lives and ministries. God always gives His servants power equal
to the work He asks of them. There are difficult times in this work
of casting out Satan from his strongholds. Pray that everyone
who takes part in it may receive and act in the power of the Holy
Spirit. Think of the specific difficulties of your missionaries and
pray for them. Pray, trusting in God's faithfulness. "God can be
trusted to keep his promise. . . . [Sarah] believed that God would
keep his promise" (Hebrews 10:23; 11:11).

Just think about God's promises to His Son concerning His
kingdom, His promises to the church concerning the unbelievers,
and His promises to His servants concerning their work. Think
of His promises to you concerning your prayer. Then pray in the
assurance that He is faithful and only waits for prayer and faith
to fulfill them. God, who calls you to pray, is faithful; he will do
what He has promised (1 Thessalonians 5:24).

Pray for individual missionaries, making yourself one with
them, until you know that you are heard. Begin to live for Christ's
kingdom as the one thing worth living for!

*Lord, I pray for every person out on the mission field. As these
precious souls cross my mind, I ask that You pour out Your Spirit
on them in such a way that they cannot contain it. Let them
experience continuous, refreshing reminders of Your love. Amen.*

More Workers

"So pray to the Lord who is in charge of the harvest;
ask him to send more workers into his fields."

MATTHEW 9:38

It is remarkable that Jesus seeks help from His disciples in getting the need for workers supplied. What an honor put upon prayer. It is also proof that God wants prayer and will hear it.

Pray for students in theological seminaries and Bible schools that God will prepare them and send them out. Pray that all believers may be ready to go or to pray for those who go.

Pray by faith, doubting nothing. "Jesus said to the disciples, 'Have faith in God. I tell you the truth, you can say to this mountain, "May you be lifted up and thrown into the sea," and it will happen. But you must really believe it will happen and have no doubt in your heart'" (Mark 11:22-23).

Have faith in God! Ask Him to make Himself known to you as the faithful, mighty God. You will be encouraged to believe that He can give suitable and sufficient workers, however impossible this seems. But remember, He does so in answer to prayer and faith. Apply this to every opening where a good worker is needed. The work is God's. He can give the right person, but He must be asked.

Lord, I pray for the workers currently in the mission field
and those just getting ready to go out. Supply them with
what they need—spirit, mind, and body—to accomplish
the great work You have placed on their hearts. Amen.

Convicting the World of Sin

"I will send [the Advocate] to you. And when
he comes, he will convict the world of its sin."
JOHN 16:7-8

The one object of Christ's coming was to take away sin. The first work of the Spirit in the world is conviction of sin. Without that, no real conversion is possible. Pray that the Gospel may be preached in such power that men may see they have rejected and crucified Christ and come to know His saving grace.

Pray most earnestly for a mighty power of conviction of sin wherever the Gospel is preached.

Take hold of God's strength when you pray. Read what Isaiah wrote. "Let him take hold of my strength, that he may make peace with me" (Isaiah 27:5 KJV). "Yet no one calls on your name or pleads with you for mercy" (Isaiah 64:7). Paul adds, "Fan into flames the spiritual gift God gave you" (2 Timothy 1:6).

First, take hold of God's strength. God is a spirit. I cannot take hold of Him except by the Spirit. Take hold of God's strength and hold on until He has done for you what He has promised.

Second, by the Holy Spirit's power in you, fan the flames of intercession in you. Give your whole heart and will to it.

Lord, I relentlessly intercede for the lost. I pray they would
hear the Gospel shared in such a way that they would
experience Your saving grace and feel compelled to
receive Your gift of salvation. Amen.

The Spirit of Burning

The Lord will...cleanse...with the
hot breath of fiery judgement.
ISAIAH 4:4

A washing by fire! A cleansing by judgment! Those who have passed through this will be called holy. The power of intercession and blessing for the world depends upon the spiritual state of the church.

Judgment must begin at the house of God; there must be conviction of sin for sanctification. Plead with God to give His Spirit as a spirit of judgment and a spirit of burning—to discover and burn out sin in His people.

Pray in the name of Christ, for He said, "You can ask for anything in my name, and I will do it.... Yes, ask me for anything in my name, and I will do it!" (John 14:13-14).

Ask in the name of your Redeemer God who sits upon the throne. Ask what He has promised—what He gave His blood for—that sin may be put away from among His people. Ask—the prayer is after His own heart—for the spirit of deep conviction of sin to come to His people. Ask for the spirit of burning. Ask in the faith of His name—the faith of what He will and of what He can do. Then look for the answer. Pray that the church may be blessed and be a blessing in the world.

Lord, give us a cleansing by fire. May the fire of
the Holy Spirit purge all that is impure and ungodly
from our hearts. Let the void of what is removed be
filled with a holy passion for relationship with You. Amen.

The Church of the Future

Then [each generation] will not be like their
ancestors—stubborn, rebellious, and unfaithful,
refusing to give their hearts to God.

PSALM 78:8

Pray for the next generation who are to come after us. Isaiah wrote, "I will pour out my Spirit on your descendants" (Isaiah 44:3). Think of the young men and young women and children today and pray for all the special organizations that work with them. Pray that wherever they are Christ may be honored and the Holy Spirit gets possession of them.

Pray with your whole heart. "May [the LORD] grant your heart's desires" (Psalm 20:4). "You have given him his heart's desire" (Psalm 21:2). "I pray with all my heart; answer me, LORD!" (Psalm 119:145). God listens to every request with His whole heart. Each time we pray, the whole infinite God is there to hear. He asks that in each prayer the whole person be there, too, and that we pray with our whole heart. If once we seek God with our whole heart, the whole heart will be in every prayer with which we come to God. Pray with your whole heart for our young people.

Heavenly Father, I pray for young people today. Their world
is full of so many distractions. Pour out Your Spirit on them
and allow them to experience Your presence and Your power.
May they come to know You personally today. Amen.

Schools and Colleges

"These words I have given you. . .will be on your lips and on
the lips of your children and your children's children forever."
ISAIAH 59:21

The future of the church and the world depends on today's education. The church may be seeking to evangelize unbelievers but is giving up her own children to secular and materialistic influences. Pray for schools and colleges and for godly teachers. The church also has a duty to care for her children.

Do not limit God in your prayers. It is a fearful thing to do so. "They tested God's patience and provoked the Holy One of Israel" (Psalm 78:41). Jesus "did only a few miracles there because of their unbelief" (Matthew 13:58). However, apart from such unbelief, God is not limited. "Is anything too hard for the LORD?" (Genesis 18:14). "O Sovereign LORD! You made the heavens and earth by your strong hand and powerful arm. Nothing is too hard for you! . . . I am the LORD. . . . Is anything too hard for me?" (Jeremiah 32:17, 27).

Beware of limiting God in your prayer, not only by unbelief but also by pretending that you know what He can do. Expect unexpected things, greater than all we ask or think. Each time you intercede, be quiet first and worship God. Acknowledge what He can do and expect great things.

God, Your Word promises You will do abundantly above all
that I could imagine. I have great expectations for the next
generation. I worship You, and I praise You for the exceedingly
great work You are doing even as I pray! Amen.

Sunday Schools

"The captives of warriors will be released, and the plunder of tyrants will be retrieved. For I will fight those who fight you, and I will save your children."

ISAIAH 49:25

Every part of the work of God's church is His work. He must do it. Prayer is acknowledging that He will. It is the surrender of ourselves into His hands to let Him work in us and through us. Pray for hundreds of thousands of Sunday school teachers who know God that they may be filled with His Spirit. Pray for your own Sunday school. Pray for the salvation of the children.

Pray boldly. "We have a great High Priest. . .Jesus the Son of God. . . . So let us come boldly to the throne of our gracious God" (Hebrews 4:14, 16).

As we have been thinking about the work of intercession, what is it doing for us? Does it make us aware of our weakness in prayer? Thank God for this. It is the very first lesson we need on the way to praying the "earnest prayer of a righteous person [that] has great power and produces wonderful results" (James 5:16). Let us persevere in taking each item boldly to the throne of grace. As we pray, we shall learn to pray, to believe, and to expect with increasing boldness. Hold fast your confidence; it is at God's command you come as an intercessor. Christ will give you grace to pray as you should.

God, all that happens in the church is Your work. What You have promised You will do. Fill every Sunday school teacher with Your Spirit and empower those men and women to bring children to a full understanding of relationship with Jesus Christ. Amen.

Kings and Rulers

Pray for all people. Ask God to help them; intercede
on their behalf, and give thanks for them.

1 TIMOTHY 2:1

Our text is an example of real faith in the power of prayer! A few weak and despised Christians are to influence the mighty Roman emperors and help secure peace and quietness. Prayer is a power that is honored by God in His rule of the world. Let us pray for our country and its rulers, for all the rulers of the world, for rulers in cities or districts in which we are interested. When God's people unite, they can count upon their prayer affecting the unseen world more than they know.

Prayer is an incense before God. "Then another angel with a gold incense burner came and stood at the altar. And a great amount of incense was given to him to mix with the prayers of God's people as an offering on the gold altar before the throne. The smoke of the incense, mixed with the prayers of God's holy people, ascended up to God from the altar where the angel had poured them out. Then the angel filled the incense burner with fire from the altar and threw it down upon the earth; and thunder crashed, lightning flashed, and there was a terrible earthquake" (Revelation 8:3–5).

The same incense burner brings the prayers of the saints before God and throws fire upon the earth. The prayers that go up to heaven have their share in the history of this earth. Be assured that your prayers enter God's presence.

God, I come to You on behalf of world leaders. I join
my faith and prayers with other believers who are
concerned for our world. Pour out Your presence; speak
to these leaders; reveal Yourself to them, I pray. Amen.

Pray for Peace

[The LORD] causes wars to end throughout the earth.
PSALM 46:9

The military armaments in which the nations find their pride are a terrible sight! The evil passions that may at any moment bring on war are a terrible thought! The suffering and desolation that come from war are a sad prospect!

"I urge you, first of all, to pray. . .for kings and all who are in authority so that we can live peaceful and quiet lives marked by godliness and dignity. This is good and pleases God our Savior" (1 Timothy 2:1–3). God can, in answer to the prayer of His people, give peace. Let us pray for it and for the rule of righteousness.

When you pray, pray with understanding. "I will pray in the spirit, and I will also pray in words I understand" (1 Corinthians 14:15). We need to pray in the Spirit if we are to take hold of God in faith and power. We need to pray with understanding if we are really to enter deeply into the needs we bring before Him. Be careful to understand the nature, the extent, the urgency of the request. Comprehend the certainty of God's promise as revealed in His Word. Let the mind affect the heart. Pray with understanding and in the Spirit.

God, I pray for peace. I pray for leaders across the land to rule in righteousness. Give wisdom and peace to our leadership and strength to those in the midst of the battle. Amen.

The Mistake

"Remain in me, and I will remain in you."
JOHN 15:4

A person thinks, *I have my business, family, and community responsibilities. In addition, I am to serve God in order to keep from sin. I hope God will help me.*

That is not right. When Christ came, He bought you with His blood. In those days, there was slavery. If someone bought a slave, the slave was required to take orders from his master. The slave lived as if he had no will or interests of his own. His one responsibility was to promote the well-being of his master.

In a similar manner, I have been purchased with the blood of Christ. I am to live every day with one thought: *How can I please my Master?*

We find the Christian life so difficult because we seek God's blessing while we live life according to our own desires. We make our own plans and choose our own work. Then we ask the Lord to help us not to go too far wrong. Instead, our relationship with Jesus should be that we are entirely at His disposal. We should ask Him daily, "Lord, is there anything in me that is not according to Your will, that is not entirely surrendered to You?"

If we will wait patiently for His guidance, there will spring up a relationship between us and Christ so close that we will be amazed. He will take actual possession of us and give us unbroken fellowship.

Lord, help me to live a life of service to You. If there is anything in my life that is not wholly surrendered to You, please reveal it and help me to make the necessary adjustments. Thank You, Jesus. Amen.

The Unreached

"See, my people will return from far away,
from. . .as far south as Egypt."
ISAIAH 49:12

Will the unreached come to Christ? Does God have such a plan? "Let Egypt come with gifts of precious metals; let Ethiopia bow in submission to God" (Psalm 68:31). "At the right time, I, the LORD, will make it happen" (Isaiah 60:22).

Pray for those who are yet without the Word: China with its hundreds of millions without Christ, India with its millions and millions each year living in darkness. If Christ gave His life for them, you can give yourself up to intercede for them.

If you have not started to intercede, begin now. God's Spirit will draw you on. Persevere, however hesitant you are. Ask God to give you some country or people group to pray for. Can anything be nobler than to do as Christ did—to give your life for the unreached?

Pray with confident expectation of an answer. "Ask me and I will tell you remarkable secrets you do not know about things to come" (Jeremiah 33:3). "This is what the Sovereign LORD says: I am ready to hear Israel's prayers" (Ezekiel 36:37). Both texts refer to promises definitely made, but their fulfillment would depend upon prayer.

Almighty God, send Your presence to every part of the
earth. Minister to those who have not yet heard the truth
of the great sacrifice made on their behalf so they
may receive Your gift of eternal life. Amen.

God's Spirit on Israel

"Then I will pour out a spirit of grace and prayer on the family of David and on the people of Jerusalem. They will look on me whom they have pierced."

ZECHARIAH 12:10

"Dear brothers and sisters, the longing of my heart and my prayer to God is for the people of Israel to be saved" (Romans 10:1). Paul states his desire for the well-being of Israel. Pray for them. Their return to the God of their fathers stands connected, in a way we cannot understand, with wonderful blessing to the church and with the coming of our Lord Jesus. Don't think that God has foreordained all this and that we cannot hasten it. In a divine and mysterious way, God has connected the fulfillment of His promise with our prayer. His Spirit's intercession in us is God's forerunner of blessing. Pray for Israel and the work done among them. Pray, too: "Amen! Come, Lord Jesus!" (Revelation 22:20). Pray with the intercession of the Holy Spirit. "We don't know what God wants us to pray for. But the Holy Spirit prays for us with groanings that cannot be expressed in words" (Romans 8:26).

In our ignorance and weakness, we can believe in the secret intercession of the Holy Spirit within us. Habitually yield yourself to His life and leading. He will help your weakness in prayer. Plead the promises of God even where you do not see how they are to be fulfilled. God knows the mind of the Spirit because "the Spirit pleads for us believers in harmony with God's own will" (Romans 8:27). Pray with the simplicity of a little child; pray with the holy awe and reverence of one in whom God's Spirit dwells and prays.

God, I plead and intercede for the Jewish nation—Your chosen people. For those who do not know Jesus as Messiah, open their eyes and hearts that they may know Christ. Amen.

The Suffering

Remember also those being mistreated,
as if you felt their pain in your own bodies.
HEBREWS 13:3

We live in a world of suffering! The persecuted believers in Islamic countries, the famine-stricken millions, those in poverty and wretchedness, refugees from armed conflict—and so much more. In our smaller circles, in thousands of homes and hearts, there is great sorrow. In our own neighborhood, how many need help or comfort? Let us have a heart for the suffering. Jesus sacrificed all and identified Himself with our suffering. Let us in our measure do so, too. It will stir us to pray, to work, to hope, to love more. And in a way and time we do not understand, God will hear our prayers.

Pray always without giving up. "Jesus told his disciples a story to show that they should always pray and never give up" (Luke 18:1).

Have you begun to feel that prayer is really the help needed for this sinful world? The very greatness of the task makes us despair! What can our ten minutes of intercession accomplish? It is okay that we feel this; it may be the way in which God is calling and preparing us to give more of our time to prayer. Give yourself wholly to God, pour out your heart to others in love, and look to God in dependence and expectation. To a heart thus led by the Holy Spirit, it is possible to pray always and not give up.

Jesus, give me a heart of compassion for those suffering
in our world today. I depend on You to show me how to
intercede for these souls. I refuse to give up, and will
hold on to hope that they will come to know You! Amen.

The Spirit in Your Own Work

*That's why I work and struggle so hard, depending on
Christ's mighty power that works within me.*

COLOSSIANS 1:29

You have your own special work; make it a work of intercession. Paul worked hard, depending on God's power working in him. Remember, God not only created us but works in us. You can do your work only in His strength—by Him working in you through the Spirit.

Intercede often for those you work with and for other believers, too. Pray in God's very presence. "Come close to God, and God will come close to you" (James 4:8).

The nearness of God gives rest and power in prayer. The nearness of God is given to those who make it their first aim to "come close to God." Seek His nearness, and He will give it. He "will come close to you." Then it becomes easy to pray in faith.

Remember that when first God takes you into the school of intercession, it is almost more for your own sake than for that of others. You have to be trained to love and wait and pray and believe. Only persevere. Learn to place yourself in His presence, to wait quietly for the assurance that He draws near. Enter His holy presence, wait there, and bring your concerns before Him.

*Lord, I love Your presence. I want to be with You. I seek You
earnestly as I pray. Speak to my heart and reveal Your
thoughts. Teach me to pray without ceasing. Amen.*

The Local Church

"Beginning in Jerusalem."
LUKE 24:47

Most of us are connected with some church congregation—a community of believers. They are to us the part of Christ's body with which we come into most direct contact. They have a special claim on our intercession. Let it be a settled matter between God and you that you are to intercede on their behalf. Pray for the minister and all leaders and workers. Pray for the believers according to their needs. Pray for conversions. Pray for the power of the Spirit to manifest itself. Join with others in specific prayer. Let intercession be a definite work, carried on as systematically as preaching or Bible studies. And pray, expecting an answer.

Pray continually. Read the scriptures. "Watchmen. . .will pray day and night. . . . Take no rest, all you who pray" (Isaiah 62:6). ". . .his chosen people who cry out to him day and night" (Luke 18:7). "Night and day we pray earnestly for you" (1 Thessalonians 3:10). "Now a true widow, a woman who is truly alone in this world, has placed her hope in God. She prays night and day, asking God for his help" (1 Timothy 5:5).

When the glory of God and the love of Christ and the needs of others are revealed to us, the fire of this unceasing intercession will begin to burn in us for those who are near and those who are far away.

God, like a watchman on the wall protecting the city,
I plead with You for my church. I pray for our church
leadership and those in our congregation. May we love one
another and reach out to new believers with Your love! Amen.

The Salvation of Souls

Therefore he is able, once and forever, to save those who come to God through him. He lives forever to intercede with God on their behalf.

HEBREWS 7:25

Christ's power to save depends on unceasing intercession. "Then we apostles can spend our time in prayer and teaching the word . . . . God's message continued to spread. The number of believers greatly increased" (Acts 6:4, 7). After the apostles spent time away in continual prayer, the number of the disciples multiplied greatly.

As we spend time in intercession, we will see more conversions. Christ is exalted as sinners repent. The church exists with the divine purpose and promise of conversions. Don't be ashamed to confess your sin and weakness and pray to God for more conversions both here and in other countries. Plead for the salvation of sinners. Pray in deep humility. "That's true, Lord, but even dogs are allowed to eat the scraps. . . ." "Dear woman . . . your faith is great. Your request is granted" (Matthew 15:27–28).

True humility proves its integrity by not seeking anything but simply trusting His grace. And so it is the strength of a great faith. Don't let your littleness hinder you for a moment.

Lord, I ask for more souls to come to know You. Move their hearts with Your Spirit. I humbly stand before You, trusting that Your grace will move in hearts and compel those who are lost to receive Your precious gift of salvation. Amen.

Young Converts

As soon as [Peter and John] arrived, they prayed
for these new believers to receive the Holy Spirit.
The Holy Spirit had not yet come upon any of them.
ACTS 8:15–16

Many new converts remain weak, many fall into sin, and many backslide entirely. As you pray for the church, its growth in holiness and devotion to God, pray especially for the young converts. Many stand alone, surrounded by temptation. Many have no teaching on the Spirit in them and the power of God to establish them. They don't know the promise of scripture: "It is God who enables us, along with you, to stand firm for Christ. . . . He has identified us as his own by placing the Holy Spirit in our hearts" (2 Corinthians 1:21–22). Many are in other countries, surrounded by Satan's power. Pray for the power of the Spirit in the church and especially that every young convert may know the fullness of the Spirit.

Pray without ceasing. "As for me, I will certainly not sin against the LORD by ending my prayers for you" (1 Samuel 12:23).

It is sin against the Lord to stop praying for others. Once we begin to see how indispensable intercession is—just as much a duty as loving God—we will feel that to stop intercession is sin. Ask for grace to fill the role of intercessor with joy and give your life to bring down the blessings of heaven.

Lord, I pray for new converts and those who are immature
in their faith. Bring mentors and teachers into their lives
who will disciple them. Let them be receptive to the
wisdom of their teachers, in Your name! Amen.

Realize Our Calling

"I will bless you and. . .you will be a blessing to others. . . .
All the families on earth will be blessed through you."
Genesis 12:2–3

Abraham was only blessed that he might be a blessing to all the earth. Israel prays for blessing that God may be known among all nations. Every believer, just as much as Abraham, is blessed so that he may carry God's blessing to the world. "May God be merciful and bless us. May his face smile with favor on us. May your ways be known throughout the earth, your saving power among people everywhere" (Psalm 67:1–2).

Plead with God that His people may know that every believer is only to live for the interests of God and His kingdom. If this truth were preached and believed and practiced, it would bring dramatic changes in our mission work. We would have a host of willing intercessors.

Pray as one who has accepted for himself what he asks for others. "The Holy Spirit fell on them, just as he fell on us at the beginning. . . . God gave these Gentiles the same gift he gave us" (Acts 11:15, 17).

As you pray for the Holy Spirit to take entire possession of God's people for God's service, yield yourself to God and claim the gift anew in faith. As the blessing comes to others, you, too, will be helped.

Father God, possess Your people for Your service.
May every believer live for You and Your kingdom—
not for their own selfish purposes. I wholly give
myself to You. Use me for Your service today. Amen.

Know the Holy Spirit

*Don't you realize that your body
is the temple of the Holy Spirit?*

1 CORINTHIANS 6:19

The Holy Spirit is the power of God for the salvation of men. He only works as He dwells in the church. He is given to enable believers to live as God wants them to live—in the full experience and witness of Him who saves completely.

Ask God for every one of His people to know the Holy Spirit! They cannot expect to live as their Father desires without having Him in His fullness, without being filled with Him! Pray that all God's people may learn to say: "I believe in the Holy Spirit."

Pray earnestly. "Epaphras, a member of your own fellowship . . .sends you his greetings. He always prays earnestly for you, asking God to make you strong and perfect, fully confident of the whole will that you are following God" (Colossians 4:12).

To a healthy man, work is a delight; he works earnestly in what interests him. The believer who is in good spiritual health, whose heart is filled with God's Spirit, prays earnestly. For what?—that believers may stand perfect and complete in all the will of God, that they may know what God wills for them and walk by the Holy Spirit.

*God, I pray that each and every human being be filled
with a great desire to experience the presence of Your
Spirit. I hope and trust in You, as I embrace instruction
of the Holy Spirit in my heart. Amen.*

The Spirit of Intercession

*"I chose you. I appointed you to go and produce
lasting fruit, so that the Father will give you
whatever you ask for, using my name."*

JOHN 15:16

Often our intercession lacks power because we have not prayed in the name of Jesus. He promised His disciples that when the Holy Spirit came upon them, they could ask for anything in His name. Let us intercede today for all God's children that Christ may teach them that the Holy Spirit is in them. May He teach us what it is to live in His fullness and to yield ourselves to His work of intercession within us. The church and the world need nothing as much as a mighty Spirit of intercession to bring down the power of God on earth. Pray for the Spirit of intercession to bring a great prayer revival.

Pray, joined to Christ. "If you remain in me and my words remain in you, you may ask for anything you want, and it will be granted!" (John 15:7).

Our acceptance with God—our access to Him—is all in Christ. As we consciously abide in Him, we have the liberty to ask what we will in the power of the new nature, and it will be done.

*Christ Jesus, I give myself to You. Teach me to live in
Your fullness and walk the path You have set before me.
Show me Your ways as I put on the power of the
new nature I have through You! Amen.*

Scripture Index